Secret Traces of the Soul of Mileva Maric-Einstein

by

Svetlana Alter

DORRANCE PUBLISHING CO., INC.
PITTSBURGH, PENNSYLVANIA 15222

Dorrance Publishing Co., Inc.
701 Smithfield Street
Pittsburgh, PA 15222
Visit our website at *www.dorrancebookstore.com*

ISBN: 978-1-4349-2803-0
eISBN: 978-1-4349-2155-0

Introduction

This novel arose from the embodied belief about the magnificent shadows of the ancient times, which flew up to the "Olympic Heights" and suddenly settled into my soul, becoming the integral part of my inalienable reality, the restless force of the destiny of my own self.

The inner voice came from the infinite archaic thread of the past reality uttered through the form of words of Mila Aleckovic-Nikolic, a doctor of psychology who in her talks expressed the need for enlightening the character and the deed of the great, intelligent Serbian woman, Mileva Marić-Einstein.

Deep inside I felt the divine wisdom that entered the course of my thoughts, changing the contours of life of this mysterious personality of Mileva Marić-Einstein.

It was the inner need that nothing should be left unrevealed, unspoken, that truth must be brought to life about the people and their secret "cosmic bonds," the people who were hidden from the world's eyes so far.

Nothing is accidental in this novel; everything came spontaneously as if being the outcome of a strange magic mission, whose task was to enlighten the "secret traces of the soul of Mileva Marić-Einstein."

My heart was quivering while I was full of expectations and surprise, getting to know the life of the ingenious woman physicist and mathematician Mileva Marić-Einstein, realizing from the very beginning that her victory and greatness is inevitable.

Rare are the globe trotters, the masters of our scientific history who were left lost and forgotten like Mileva Marić. This bright Serbian woman coming from great Vojvodina plain remained up to the present covered with the veil of oblivion and negligence. She was wiped out of the memories, plucked from the root of the glorious world of science, forgotten from everyone, even from her own Serbs, although by her courage, energy, intelligence, and kindness, she was the one who made up the picture of the Serbian woman.

If you penetrate under the surface, you will discover the Serbian carelessness, insufficient knowledge about some other great scientists such as Tesla and Pupin, who were found better sanctuary under the wing of world civilization than in their home country. All of them, particularly Mileva Marić, were the "white spots" of our past on the historical map of the mankind.

The purpose of this book is to enliven the hidden work, mysterious truth unknown to the world. Mileva Marić-Einstein pops up as the myth in all its greatness, mocking at our ignorance and our carelessness. Her life and her love had some other features and values. "Everything in an internal world was arranged according to the quality of measures and ratio, inevitably forming beauty and elegance," says Plato. Mileva, united with love bonds with Albert Einstein, was staring at the infinity that took them into the land of the unknown, to the state of perfection, giving the world a gift, the Theory of Relativity.

Mileva Marić tied her ingenious mind with her love towards her colleague, Albert Einstein. He was the man of her life, her irrational power, the world harmony that lived forever in herself, making the synthesis of the best human virtues in Mileva's spiritual postulate.

She accepted the eternal love as the main guideline in her life and in space. She lived her life beyond the conventional forms of space and time. The two ingenious minds were interwoven by destiny, the mind of Albert Einstein, the physicist, and the mathematician, Mileva Marić, with the permanent tie that would remain a secret, because it was covered by the veil of the romantic love legend of the pure Mileva's soul who, till the rest of her life, remained enchanted with her beloved husband.

Whatever standard you use to judge and estimate this scientific couple, you will realize that they deserve the greatest glory in the history of the science world. You may wonder, correctly, why the illusory colours of temporariness have not been taken off so far. Why have the miraculous truth and numerous evidence of Mileva's scientific work been taken to the other side of this world? Why?

Today, I am torn between the question and the answer, between the eternal truth and treacherous words of an ordinary man. I am wandering across the Vojvodina fields. I can feel strange peace and human kindness.

"Now I know; she was the one who wanted me to feel all that."

In the breeze of the autumn wind, I can hear her words, quietly as the whispering of the yellow leaves of the big tree in front of her house.

"My soul and science belong forever to my beloved Albert, whereas my mortal body belongs to the fertile Vojvodina plain, and therefore I want to return to the mound under the poplars."

There she stood, before my eyes, as if brought there by fate itself, as if resurrected, our first physicist, the ingenious Mileva Marić-Einstein. I felt strange happiness, security, and tranquility. The justice might be satisfied today. It may be.

If you come to a halt on your life path, I am sure that you will, just like me, hear the words of Mileva Marić-Einstein, and then you will open the gate of glory and realize the scientific guidance, its power, because it represents the "myth of a Serbian woman."

The science-based novel titled *Secret Traces of the Soul of Mileva Marić-Einstein* is a story about a woman scientist, guided by strange forces that enchanted her, deceived her, taking her to the longing love that would live beyond the time. It is a story about an ordinary woman and the rule of the eternal natural law of man, the law of the mightier, that defeats even an eternal love. She lived her life as an active participant, sincerely, through others. All her life was a drama played for others. This ingenious person, certainly one of the most distinguished women in the world, deserves to enter the scientific history shoulder to shoulder with Albert Einstein.

Mileva Marić-Einstein, by her scientific greatness and extraordinary eternal love, deserves to gain the honorary place in the heart of the world. Therefore, my dear readers, open the doors of your souls! Let the divine, eternal light of love enter your souls, the light called Mileva Marić-Einstein! She left us a message, saying that she was leaving, but also that she would be back again.

This may be the moment of her return!

This may be the moment when the myth is entering history!

I would like to tell you one of my theories about Mileva…
The theory is called "The Drawn Arrow".

The life path of Mileva seems to me like the path of the arrow drawn from the bow, which was getting strained in her youth so much that it simply broke. Once it flew upwards into great heights, there was no return.

Academic and intellectual life became her great love.

Dr Rastko Maglic,
Teacher from Colorado University
Colorado Springs, USA.

AMIDST THAT UNKNOWN WORLD UNDER THE ENCHANTINGLY DAZZLING CANOPY

"Tell me about the past, and I will know the future."

Confucius

In the year 1875 on the 7th of December,
the bright heaven opened above Titel.
In silence, one soul, guided by destiny,
shifts into earthly life.
It is the soul of the child, just being delivered,
the soul of Mileva Marić.

It was one of those frosty-grey nights that was drifting slowly, almost soundlessly, softly touching the roofs of the houses in Titel, fallen asleep in the white magic of the winter dream.

All 'round, the glass woven-in frosty icicles dazzle in the pale moonlight as if the diamonds were dropped from a distant, already-told fairytale.

In such a cold and bright night, when the human's breath changes into misty frost, and the snow drift reaches more than three feet upward, the maid from the Marićs' house knocked at the front door of the house of the country house of a delivery nurse Ana Koncek, a widow from Titel, hastily sent her a message: to come immediately to the Marićs' farm, because, she said, it was very urgent; the lady had been having delivery pains since the previous night.

When the delivery nurse received the message, still sleepy, she began dressing up quickly. She came to the basin, splashed her face with water, especially her eyes, in order to awake as soon as possible, and put her wet hair in order with her wet hands. At that moment a big clock with heavy weights clang: *Bang, bang!* and ticked bluntly the first five morning hours. The nurse put on her leather sheepskin coat hastily, put on her wooden clogs filled with straw, fetched a big black bag full of instruments, and left out into the cold winter morning with haste. Outside stood the sledges filled with straw piled up to the top, in which Marić's driver and the maid were waiting for her. The driver took off the blanket in which he was wrapped and covered the nurse.

"It will be warmer in this way," he mumbled. "This damned snow."

"It's cold tonight," she said, taking a seat on the sledges.

The maid sat in the middle between the nurse and the driver so that she could mutter, talk, and grumble so that both of them may hear her well. She kept talking about the salas during the drive, about the hard delivery pains of Mrs Marija, about how she would ask for the nurse even last night, but nobody listened to her. Then, she began hurrying the driver to drive the black horses faster, who were snorting, making their way through the snowdrifts.

At daybreak the decorated sledges of the nobleman were gliding quickly, whereas the harness with the jingles, which kept shaking, melodically, tenderly, and mildly echoing through the empty Vojvodina plain. December morning was bright and cold. On the grey horizon, a dim light was emerging from the Marićs' farm.

In front of the house, impatiently, Mr Marić was waiting, with a painful expression on his face, hurrying the nurse from afar, until the sledges did not reach the house, saying, "Here it is, here is the room of the woman with labor pains...."

The nurse almost ran into the big house from which terrible delivery cries were thundering. Marić was left alone on the porch. As stiff as the shadow, he was staring at the snow-covered field and catching his breath, drowning himself into the pain and fear for his wife and the child. Everything seemed too long for him, and he became increasingly overwhelmed by the impatience and fear. It has been almost two hours since the nurse entered the house. His heart was sinking. He was overcome with worry, which made him walk up and down the porch nervously.

All of a sudden, a sharp, loud crying of the child was heard. Milos jerked as if awoken from sleep and ran into the house. At the door he ran into a nurse, who was wiping sweat from her forehead. He looked at her curiously.

"It was very hard, but they are both well now, thank God," said the nurse.

Marić could hardly make out the uttered words. Being out of himself with joy, he ran into the room to see his wife and the newborn.

The newborn child was the third child of Milos Marić (the son of Kuzman and Moja), a lower officer of the Sajkas battalion, who was born at Kac in 1846, and Marija Ruzic from Titel, a daughter of a well-to-do farmer. They got married in 1867. The first two children, Milica and Vukasin, died several years upon their birth.

The newborn girl had pitch-black hair, wide-open eyes, and a strong wish for food and life.

For a moment, by her presence, she caused a real mess in the house. All around you could hear joyful cries and hasty running of the maids. The relatives began arriving, embracing each other, congratulating and blessing the newborn child. The maids brought out a hot brandy, and all of them were making a toast, breaking the glasses and wishing luck and good health to the newborn child.

It happened on a sunny morning of the 7th of December (19 December), 1875, on the day of Saint Amvrosije, the magician and holy wise man. The newborn girl was blessed with the wisdom of this saint.

The next day, upon the birth of the child, on the 8th of December, at the church of Resurrection of the Holy Virgin, the girl was Christened by Titel's priest, Atanasije Popovic. Blessed be little girl! Her godmother at the Christening was Jelena Zoric. Mileva was born in the country (Titel, Serbia), at the Marićs' home, the home of a well-to-do family owning great deal of property.

The Marić family had come from Serbia, in one of the migrations, to the border between Austro-Hungary and Turkey. It was first mentioned at Kac, in the population records from 1720. The founder of the Backa's family origin was Marko Marić.

The grandfather, Milos Marić, had been a lower village clerk in the village of Kac. "Kac is a village in the vicinity of Novi Sad, but it belonged to Sajkas community: It had 2564 Serbian inhabitants, 168 Lutheran and 21 Rome-Catholic inhabitants," records Djordje Krstic.

For a long time, Titel's region had been a military area. Titel's region had been populated by Samaritans during the Roman period. The Romans had built there a military station, a look-out, a protruding point on the defence line, which was protecting the Roman Empire from the Barbarians. At the time of the weakening of the Roman Empire, when the state defence power had been decreasing, the region was invaded by the Huns and Avars.

On the Tite's hill of Kalvarija, a pagan leader, Attila, called "Attila the Hun," had placed his troops so that he could attack glorious Sirmium.

Titel was first mentioned in the written records in 1138, which recorded that "Titel was a military fortification with towers and fortified walls."

When Belgrade had fallen under the Turkish rule (in 1521), the importance of Titel's fortress increased. From 1736 to 1873, Titel had been the seat of the Sajkas battalion of the river crew (Danubian), a war fleet made of Saajkas (small boats), which had the task to protect the Potiska military border. The soldiers had many privileges and had the right to practice trade and farming with no taxes. The Serbs proved to be good soldiers, so they made the majority of the Austrian army in Vojvodina. The whole area of Backa got the name of "Sajkas." In 1858, Titel had a famous battalion school where lectures were held in German. It was attended mostly by young men from the Sajkas region. His Majesty granted scholarships for the school to be allocated from the border financial funds. Milos Marić also attended this school and became a lower officer of the Sajkas battalion. He started his schooling in Karlovci, continued it in Novi Sad, then in Titel he finished the "tematika," that is, the subofficer's battalion school. His parents had died early, so Milos Marić heartily decided to join the army. After his marriage to Marija Ruzic, who came from a rich family from Titel, Milos would spend all his free time in Titel, at Maria's parents'. According to one record of Djordje Krstic, "in 1871 Milos, with his wife, Maria, and his son, Vukasin, left the Marić's family house number 205 with the inheritance and moved into the house of the Strangar family." This family had been recorded in Kac in 1819. In the cadastre records for Kac in the period from 1858-1900, under Milos Strangar you can find the following fact" "hausnumer 31". Pursuant to the order of the battalion issued at number 748 of the 10th of July, 1871, Milos Marić, feldvebel, with his members of family and inheritance of 500 forints value, moved into the house and adopted the name Strangar, "recorded by Djuro Krstic, according to the paper, page 338, and at the same time he became an active member of the Strangar family." Marić accepted the old man's household and big estate and enlarged his own estate that way.

A few days before Mileva's birth, Father Milos was demobilized, after thirteen years spent in the army, and the reason for that was that the Sajkas battalion ceased to exist when the military region had been abolished.

Milos Marić was elected by a decree a "reliable supervisor at Croatian court in Vukovar." He held offices as an administrative clerk, which was made possible thanks to his excellent knowledge of German and his military tidiness. Milos could speak Hungarian because he had lived among the Germans and Hungarians, who had been living in the village of Kac since his childhood.

They stayed there for more than two years.

At the end of 1877, Marić took up a post of a scriber at the District Court in Ruma with the income of more than 500 forints a year. Mileva was then about two years old. The Marićs lived on Zeleznicka Street, where Mileva spent her early childhood.

When the girl started walking, a very unpleasant physical fault could be noticed. Namely, the girl was staggering on her left leg due to the inherent deformity: hip spraining (the girl had a congenital lucsation of the left hip). That fatal night when she was born, the doom stamped an iron cross onto the fragile girl, which she would bear for the rest of her life.

As she was growing up, she increasingly comprehended her being different from the rest, and that she had to learn to bear that burden. It might have been the reason why Father Milos would spend most of his attention and time with his lame girl, who was nicknamed Mica out of love. Mica was a lovely, smart, and very quiet girl. She slowly began accepting her physical appearance and playing with the children in the neighbourhood until one day the whole herd of children started gathering around her, loudly and spitefully uttering cries: "Mica, Mica." The frightened girl tried to get out of the circle of the bullies, but she didn't succeed. She staggered and fell down. The wild and fiery crowd started dragging her, laughing at her with cries and swearing. All of a sudden they ran away, and Mileva was left lying motionlessly, as if being without consciousness. When she recovered, she rushed into the house, crying sadly and bitterly. Her mother, Marija, laid her head tenderly on the girl's head and started caressing and comforting her lovingly, questioning her about what had happened.

"Mica, did anyone beat you? What has happened? Tell your mother."

Still sobbing, Mileva told her mother interruptedly the unpleasant incident. The children wanted to laugh at the sick girl, and her mother was under a difficult temptation: how to explain to her that she could not fight against that.

Her father, Milos, that respectable, decent man, was very touched by this event. He could feel the fear that only a father could feel for the future of his daughter and her health, as well as for her normal growing up. He was sitting by the fireplace for a long time, overwhelmed with sorrow, talking to his wife about how they could help their poor little girl.

Sudden calling and a knock at the door, followed by a bell ring, which announced guests, interrupted his thoughts. Marić was convinced that a sudden arrival of a guest would help him reveal the secret and make a decision: how and in what way to bring up his girl, Mica. The guest was his old friend from Titel, a colonel, the man who knew what the willpower and discipline meant in life.

He immediately realized that the guest had problems, so he asked him, "Is there anything that I can do to help you?"

"Deep in my heart, I deny to accept to truth, but I don't know whether there is a possibility to bring my beloved daughter, Mica, in a free state of cheerfulness and carelessness, when on my mind I hold the burden of her illness, fate-domed."

He told him, then, the incident with spoilt children from Ruma.

"My dear friend", the colonel began talking, "I can see that the only way left to bring up your daughter is to develop with her the logical spirit of the military strength and to have her turn all her lost battles into the victory over the sadness of her life. You can do that only on condition that you teach her how to develop iron will and military determination."

Marić himself realized that it was the right way, and his faith in success cheered him up. It was then that Mileva's parents got a new hope, new impulses, and new doubts because they were aware of the fact that they were those who would be responsible for bringing up the girl and forming her mind.

That unpleasant incident with the children from Ruma left trace in Mileva's heart forever. On her face it cut a deep furrow of agility determination, almost spite, which she would not lose during her lifetime. Yet since that incident, she kept to herself and did not go out very often, and her father directed her to reading books. She wasn't even four when she learnt to read, count, and add and subtract quickly by heart.

She was her father's favourite, so he wanted to give her all his knowledge.

Milos Marić could speak German and Hungarian. He was a scholar, very high, with a beautiful face and shiny, determined eyes, but what mostly attracted others to his face was his noble heart, noble demeanour, knowledge, mathematical-military logic, and patriotism. He wanted to share all his knowledge with his favourite child.

Mrs Marić was a daughter of Atanasije Ruzic, a respectable rich landowner whose ancestors came from Montenegro. The Ruzic family had three daughters: Marija, Djutka, and Jelena. Milos Marić married Maria and got a big dowry that way. Marija was a short, skinny woman, energetic but quiet, modest, bound by ethics and social standards. There was a strange tranquility and dignity around her. She would sometimes complain that her husband was devoting all his time and praise to Mileva and no one else. Milos would not care about his wife's remarks. His wish to provide Mileva the access to higher education was above everything. He did not regret spending any efforts or forints on that.

So Mileva had her private piano teacher since her early childhood. She could play the piano very well at the age of eight. The girl learnt how to fight the grief, not letting herself to become overwhelmed with it. She forgot about her sick leg, and due to proper upbringing provided to her by her parents, she began forming the self-conscience. She learnt how to guard her feelings, to accept the pain, to observe the world and herself. She wondered, "What am I doing here? Where did I come from? Where I am going?". Little by little, she became aware of the far-existing world, wondering how those distances could be measured. Could that vastness be compared to anything?

In front of their house in Ruma, a large oak tree was planted. Mica admired its mighty treetops and the tree of this giant, which could not be hugged by two people only. Through that tree, she realized how mighty the nature was. The treetops seemed to be reaching the stars and the moon, whilst the branches looked as if entangled with the clouds. All these beauties enchanted the little girl by its odd power. She would lean her head onto the rough bark and feel the strength and power of that high, giant tree, which was her first connection with the heavenly vastness. Her father and mother taught her about glorious history, wars, folk songs, dignity, tradition, and faith.

Mileva started attending the first grade of the General National School in Ruma in 1881. From her father she got one big forint wishing her luck at school. Her mother gave her a nice dress to wear and shoes made of knitted leather. On her shoulder was hung a colourful handbag holding the board, stiff chalk, and a sponge.

In her class there were forty-two other girls. She finished the class with excellent grades, under her class teacher, Jelena Stanojevic, from Lezimir. It was then that Mileva first showed her inclination towards reading books, logical conclusions, and deductions. She was the best pupil in the class.

She would spend her summer holidays in Titel at her grandparents', the Ruzics, her mother's parents. Lying on a big straw bed, Mileva comprehended for the first time the width of the heavenly vastness.

One summer night, with her beloved cousin, she was watching the starry sky. The night was bright and transparent, and you could see thousands of stars in the sky shining, twinkling a mysterious light, known only to them. That night you could clearly see those scattered, light feathers popularly known as "godfathers' stray."

"It is said that a godfather stole stray from his godfather, and that such a big sin can be seen even in the sky," said his sister.

Mileva added, "But on the other hand, I heard an ancient Greek legend, which says that the milky, misty path that can be seen among the stars was made when Junona, the mother goddess nourishing Heracles at her breast, Jupiter's son, and then, it is said that a few drops of milk were dropped onto the heave, which we today see as the Milky Way."

That night Mileva's thoughts flew up into the huge vastness, in which billions of stars were shining, and where the earth was just a tiny bit in an eternal world. It was the first contemplation of Mileva's about the mysterious, heavenly space, when the thoughts about the imaginations of the youth's ideals and reality met, something that exists apart from us. It was the moment when she discovered a new world that would free her from the fears of life.

As a pupil, she showed her extraordinary intellectual powers. She would be noticed by her exquisite talent and knowledge from mathematics, drawing, and music. The priest from Ruma was proud of the knowledge of his pupil, who showed great talent for music. So in the first grade, she already knew the complete church chanting by heart. She could calculate well, so in Kac and Titel, where she would spend her summer holidays, she would gladly help in fast counting of geese, which were supposed to be classified into particular flocks. The girl would do the adding quickly by heart.

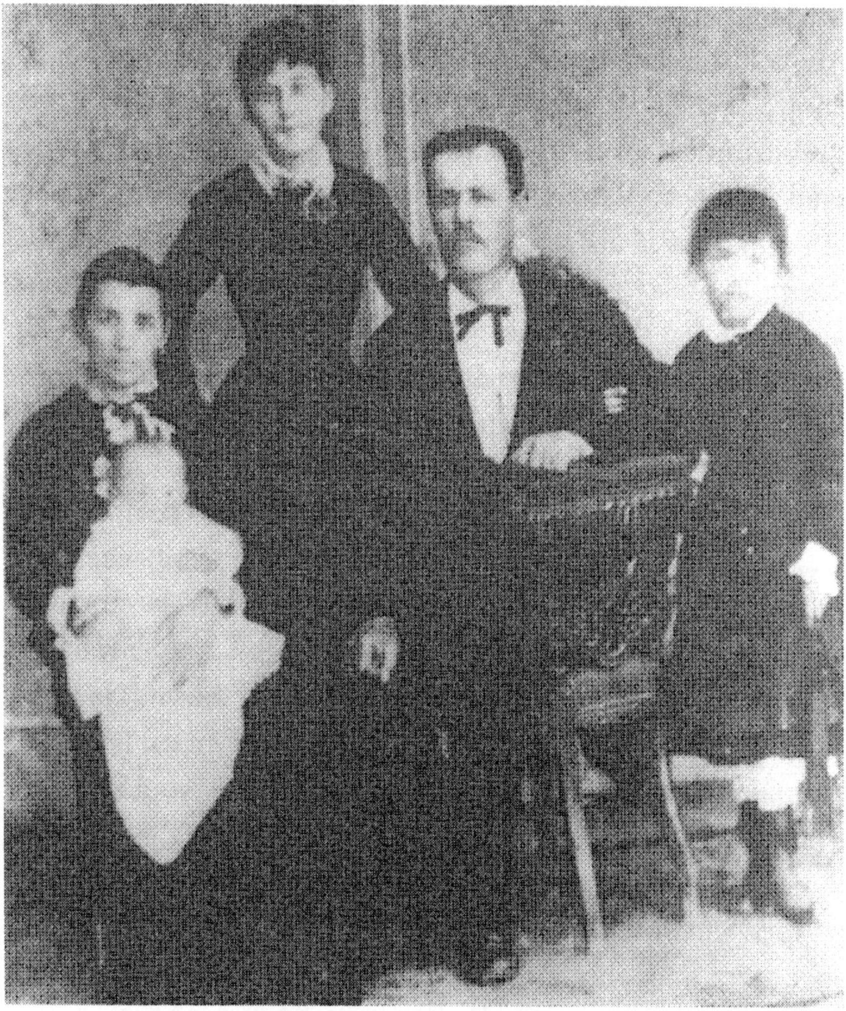

Figure No. 2: Milos Marić and Maria Ruzic with little Zorka, Mileva, and the adopted child, Nana

What also fascinated this child was the practical application of everything she had ever learnt at school. She was always searching for clear evidence and the obvious in making conclusions. Little by little, in Ruma already, Mileva began realizing the laws of nature. Her father supported her, uncovering for her the nature and the reality, not through mystery, but rather through logical thoughts. That was how she acquired a healthy spirit and accepted her own self.

In 1883 her sister, Zorka, was born, also with a damaged left hip. According to the records made by Desanka Djuric Trbuhovic, the Ruzic family came from Zeta, where such a defect would appear often. So both of the daughters were given a hard burden, which they had to wear all their life. Mileva showed great love towards her little sister and took care of her.

As a pupil, she was very hardworking. She would attend school gladly and she did not play truant. The teachers would always mention her name among those who were praised at the end of the school year. All praises, including "very diligent" and "very praiseworthy," were addressed to this wonderful, sophisticated girl, who would be distinguished by her intelligence among her classmates.

In 1885 Mileva finished the General National School in Ruma. She had a pause in the 1885/1886 school year. It was the year when her father thought that it was perhaps better for the girl to devote herself to music and to take as many piano lessons as she could. Mileva went on practising with all her heart, playing for hours. The enchanted, diligent girl had an extraordinary talent for music. However, her father soon realized that Mileva kept to herself and that she separated herself from the rest of the world. She started living only with music, in her own imaginary world. Marija and Milos were talking among themselves whether to let their girl continue the further advancement in this particular field or not. They concluded that further devotion to music would mean to her more grief and more loneliness.

It was on Sunday when the Marićs invited to lunch Avakum Spaic, a priest from Ruma, and the teacher from Karlovac High School. Father wanted them to have a close look at Mileva and estimate, together with him, how he should continue to educate this sad girl. The priest from Ruma admitted openly that never in his life had he encountered such a brilliant mind and the concentration, which was graded above average.

"I am impressed by her fast reading. I think that the moment you see her, she is able to read twenty letters." The priest would continue to praise Mileva's warm heart, which was filled with love towards all things and creatures. "She has warm feeling arising from a kind soul, expressed through her modesty and innocence, and a great ability for learning," the priest would say, praising Mileva wherever he could.

She also enjoyed listening to wonderful lectures of the priest from Ruma, who taught them how the world was created by the act of God. He used to talk warmly, as if telling a fairytale.

"In the beginning, God made heavens and earth, light and water, plants and...then God made a man out of the ashes of land and breathed life into him and there appeared a man, a living being. The man lived in the Garden of Eden, happy in abundance and love, until one day he tasted the forbidden fruit on the tree of comprehension of good and evil. Eve persuaded Adam to try the apple from the forbidden tree.

"Then, the Almighty said to the man,'You have eaten the fruit from the forbidden tree. You shall not eat from this tree. The Earth shall be damned to you. You shall not eat from the Earth in perspiration and hard work. You shall eat your bread until you come back onto the earth. You are ashes and you shall return to ashes.' There, you see," proceeded the priest, "the man was induced to sin, no one but the devil, and that is the angel antichrist, who wanted to take for himself all the power, even the power of the Almighty. We have all come to Earth to repent our sins through prayers to God and to stay away from the devil." This was how the priest from Ruma was telling the children about God, teaching them how to live justly, which Mileva would remember all her life, trying to live in a fair and honest way.

"The Almighty, by his Providence, shows us the door into that path where our soul will learn most about love, telling us to go and do not make sin. This, in some way, means that the destiny is in our hands. Then God gave us the common sense, pointing out that there are two ways: the path of the devil, the evil, the dark evil forces, and on the other hand, the path of the Christ, which is the path of light. The choice is ours." These words of the priest were taken with admiration and great interest by Mileva.

That Sunday she was sitting at the table with the guests, dressed in a light blue woolen dress with a white hand-woven collar. Her hair was tied in two short chestnut-coloured plaits, plaited with blue ribbons. She was extraordinarily beautiful and somehow strangely cheerful, listening to the wise preaching of the priest and the stories of her father and the teacher. At the Marićs' house, the table was laid for a special occasion. You could say it looked almost luxurious. Mrs Marija Marić laid that day the silver cutlery, which she had brought to the Marićs' house as her dowry. The tablecloth was hand-woven, whereas the plates were made out of top-quality Budim porcelain. There were numerous trifles on the table, a turkey and pork roasted just the way they should be, reddish as if roasted on the sun; the duck soup was delicious and yellow, with tiny chopped noodles; there were various cookies, a "pisinger" cake, honey cakes, "London cookies," a "Constantinople" cake," "pracle" cookies, vanilla cookies, "muskaconi" cookies, sour strudel with poppy and nuts, and doughnuts. For Mileva, it was a very important day. Her parents were supposed to make a decision whether to let the girl continue practising the piano or perhaps to send her to some school. However, during the whole meal, the guests were having philosophical talks about the debates that would be remembered as the brightest thoughts Mileva had ever heard in her life.

"A man must free himself from earthly hopes and worries in order to be ready to do great deeds. Some learned people claim," the priest from Karlovac went on with his story, "that a man is allowed to make his own choice so that he can live freely. On the other hand, some people say that destiny governs all our moves."

Mr Marić interfered. "The truth is somewhere in the middle."

The teacher went on quickly. "A young man, untamed by the wild strength of his energy, the youth strength, does not pay attention to natural laws and to his soul. Very often the rational conscience and its laws are suppressed and the young man makes moves by inertion, choosing the easier way, wondering along where the dead souls go, where the new souls are born from, and if there is life after death."

Mileva suddenly felt as if she were losing her breath. She was listening to the words of her teacher attentively, who then proceeded.

"The evidence, known only to us, has lasted since ancient times, that nothing ever happens by accident; everything was created according to the ancient laws of the world, so that we may not draw a border between the eternal and passing, between the natural and the unreal. The boundary is somewhere in between. Everything is interactively connected, and all that is buried deeply in one's conscious. Therefore, the question is whether we can perceive life clearly as the destiny, which is changeable and unsteady and can be seen just through the laws of the nature. The man with his sense and soul stands in the middle of that immense nature and builds life."

"It is absolutely true", said Avakum Spaic, the priest, and continued. "The human being, however powerful he may be now and till the end of time, cannot change the laws of nature. To tell the truth, he can get to know them well and use them for the benefit of mankind. Whatever we may be thinking, summer comes after spring and is followed by autumn and then winter, so the cycle goes all over again."

Marić suddenly joined them in that conversation. "A man goes through the process of development during his lifetime, following the natural path of his soul. First comes the playing and then the intellectual beginning of development, childhood, then comes the incessant act of the mature age, the age of the mind and logical conclusions, and finally the last stage of the old age, weak mumbling, sometimes even absentmindedness. It is the path of the soul of each man."

The priest interrupted his speech. "The death comes upon getting old, body ageing, whereas the soul is young and lively and it transfers invisibly from one form into another. From one life into another life. Upon its birth, it experiences a new beginning, holding in itself the ancient conscious about its eternal existence, living in this new life in new conditions and temptations, directed by waves, transformed into the deeds of the subconscious level of soul. The soul should always be progressive, to direct each of its lives towards the good, the charity, love and eternity of the God. Can we, in the set-up goal, see the shadows of our past lies? Can we perceive the eternity?

The teacher then interfered. "The laws of nature never fail; the fact is that we seldom understand our lives. Living among the number of people, we perceive them narrow-mindedly. We notice the envy, arguing, quarrels, race for money, and greed whilst we are living on earth. I hope, Father, that you will do me just that we should live the life by the eternal divine ray of heaven. Life should go on without worries, sufferings, and death pains. We are on earth out of the obvious reason, to realize that there is faith, uncertainty, and the freedom of willpower."

The priest glanced at Mileva, who opened her beautiful, big, dark brown eyes wide open, trying hard to get into memory every single uttered word. When the teacher was sure that Mileva was listening to their philosophical debate, he proceeded by telling a legend each Christian should know: to learn how to forgive the evil and hatred, which came either from his friend or from his enemy.

"The legend of the ancient nations, that each man should live in the valley of satisfaction, on the Champs Elysees, washed in the river of forgetfullness in which he should take off all the incidents and troubles that had been done to him by other people. Never, my dear, should you take revenge on your enemies. If you take revenge upon your enemies, then you call the eagle of avenger, the one that according to the legend had been pecking incessantly Prometheus, who had been tied to a rock. All the pains and trouble done to us by another man should be forgiven. Our wound, the legend says, may be cured by the balm that the Mighty Meden prepares out of magic grasses, which grow out of the bloody soul, flowed by the blood, which is leaking from Prometheus's wounds, made by the eagle the avenger. Therefore, each being should be filled with love so that the soul may be pure and perfect, whereas life then becomes one wonderful, sensible, spiritual harmony, filled with happiness and goodness. From such a person, as our Mileva was, the light fireflies of happiness shall fly in all directions, spreading all over the world the knowledge and her love towards other people."

These prophetic words would come true later in the course of Mileva's life.

Several days upon this lunch, where Mileva heard the first philosophical debates on life, soul, and happiness, Father decided to let Mileva go with her mother to Titel. It was at the time when the married couple of Marić were expecting a baby.

When they came to Titel, it was spring, a paradise for children. Numerous relatives and beauties of nature made Mileva very happy.

Titel is a village in Backa, the village of long, wide streets, dusty in summer, muddy and wet in winter so that you cannot walk freely without getting stuck in mud. In summer, whenever a poor man in a one-horse peasant cart or some aristocrats in a nice horse-drawn vehicle and a two-seater would pass along the wide dusty road, one would be almost blinded by haze, although most frequently those were the pedestrians, who would walk along the streets of Titel with movable "stores" on their backs, selling various goods.

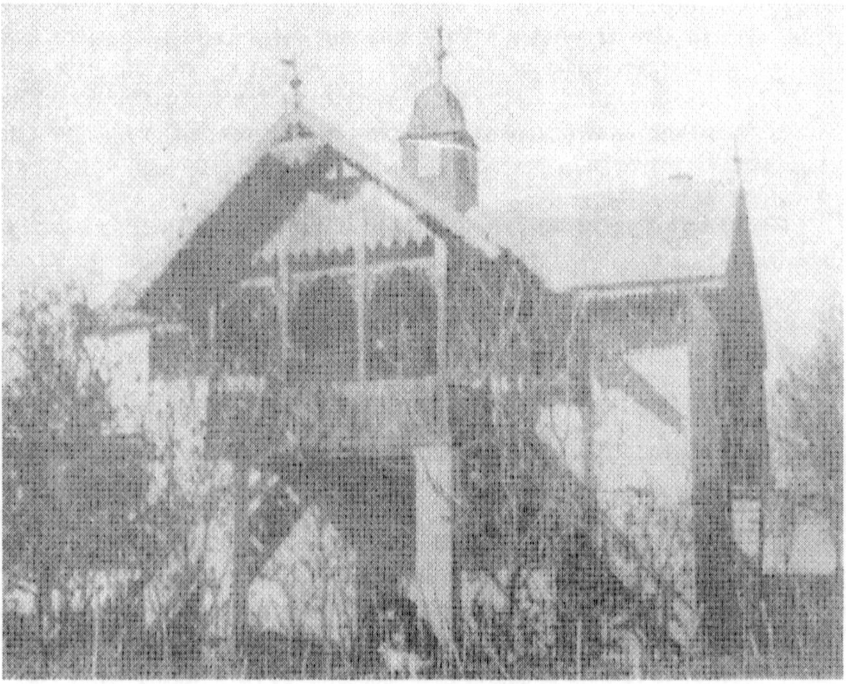

Figure 3 "The Kula" Bungalow

The Kula Bungalow. The Marićs' farm was situated not far from the village of Kac, and it was the pride of the whole Backa region. The castle, all in carvings, seemed as if coming from a fairytale. Surrounded by the hedge and wonderful park, it looked like the medieval castles from our dreams. It was spread on the two hundred hectares of land, which the servants used to cultivate.

Marić

The houses of Titel were yellowish, white, some of them greyish with high gables, whereas in front of each of them were planted mulberry trees, black and white, so that they would make good shade in summer. Almost every house had a well on winch and farm with the "djeram." Those were mostly one-story houses and under the vault with long porches from one side, whilst on the other side there lay protruded roof eaves. It was an ideal place for the children to play during warm or rainy autumn and spring days.

Mileva did not feel sad or lonely in her birthplace.

In the house, on the farm in Kula, she was happy. She was born in the region where the sun had the most beautiful colour, where love was in the scent of the mowed lawn, the creaking of the well, and the shouting of the shepherds. That spring, when she paid a visit to her grandparents, she experienced the beauty of the infinity of the Pannonian plain, where the horizon touched the eternity in a thin line. It was here that the immense fields of wheat bent in the wind, where the cultivated land had a nice scent, and the intoxicating air entered Mileva's heart and became her lucky charm that she would bear in this world.

That wonderful world, the fertile land, would never disappear from her memory. She would never forget these vivid pictures from her early childhood, and she would gladly remember them.

In the distance, by the river, there in Titel, pale green, yellowish willows can be seen. In early spring, children would make shepherd's flutes out of the willows' branches so that one could hear the loud playing, which frightened the frogs that jumped hastily into the dazzling water of the Danube branch. The river flowed through the willow lazily, calm and pure like a mirror in which the green small branches and big midday sun would bathe. When the boat found itself in the branch of the Tisa River or the Danube, you would find yourself surrounded by bamboo and willows whose branches hung above the water like the curtain with windows sheltering your view, while the white flowers of water lily peered from the water. A fish or two would pop up onto the surface as if wishing to say hello and to join the life on the shore, where white storks tread looking for food, or small barflies that mixed with the colourful big butterflies that flew over the blue, purple, and white flowers in a hurry.

It was here in Titel that Mileva felt love towards nature, and it would be a part of her for the rest of her life. Later in her life, she used to spend her free time in long walks in nature, remembering the beauty of the plain of Backa.

That spring, she got a brother, Milos, who would become her love that she felt like a lightness in her heart. She learnt how to devote all her personality to him; she would feed him, dress him, and play with him, adoring him with all her heart and soul.

Her mother, Marija, was a short and gentle woman. Whenever she would come out of the house, she would hold her husband by the hand. She respected him immensely and appreciated him; he meant everything to her. Mrs Marić Marija was a reserved and clever woman. She would have her hair tied in a bun. She had big, dark eyes that reflected perfect tranquility. She set herself a task, which was to teach Mileva how to have faith in life, in her husband, in the future, in tradition, and in God. Thus, that summer in Titel, she decided to bring up her three children and to teach Mileva, who was already a young girl, about the tradition and the faith in God. "Tradition links", she would say to her mother, Mileva, "and keep the individual character of our Serbian life, where the most appreciated values of man are the righteousness, good heartedness (the nobility or the soul), the sacrifice, as our ancestors used to say."

Mother would then talk in length about the mutual respect and friendship between parents, married couple, and children, advising her to read an old book, which was printed in 1861 and was written by Mihailo and which is called *The Church Teacher*, in which she could find various debates on the human being, on God, the God worshipping, nature, the advancement of the Christianity, morals, pride, lies, and the purity of heart.

"You can learn, Mileva, about the horrible love, wealth and death, conscious and duty, everything written in the form of speech."

Her mother would advise her with love and kindness, teaching her that love and sacrifice towards her husband was the most honourable role for one woman. Mileva blushed at these words, telling her mother that she would never marry.

Her mother would tell her about how Titel was the center of the Sajkas, that it had always been the place of not only military discipline, but religion as well. The soldiers went to fight for their home, and they would get the blessing from the priest for that. "Since ancient times, the episcope of Backa region, Josif Jovanovic Sakabent (1783–1786), gave as a gift to the Sajkas battalion in Titel the complete movable military chapel, so that each of our soldiers could pray to God and ask for mercy for the freedom of its country and the peace of its home. So while on the battlefield, the soldiers could listen to the Serbian liturgy. I will read to you about the thoughts of Vasa Pusibrk from the high school in Novi Sad, about the Serbian liturgy."

Mother began to read the thoughts of the headmaster of the high school in Novis Sad in a somewhat solemn way:

"Each real Serb enjoys the beauty of the Orthodox liturgy, and when the priest sings nicely and when the priest speaks clearly, then you are overly gracious. The man enjoys most in those church songs that he had made himself that he had adjusted through centuries according to his spirit. The Serbs shall remain the Serbs as long as they respect and love the Serbian virtues, as long as they are interested in their spiritual wealth; when all these things disappear, they themselves will disappear, too." In this way, Mileva received the first seeds of faith through her grandmother and mother, keeping them in herself not as an ordinary reverence, but rather as the form of a decent life full of faith, forming in herself the light good-heartedness.

The time spent with her mother, sister Zorka, and brother Milos in Titel that spring and summer would remain the part of her most vivid memories.

Around the beginning of the school year of 1886, her father suddenly came to Titel and asked Mileva an unavoidable question, and it was whether she would continue with music education or some other higher education.

Since that lunch in Ruma and the philosophical debates that she had listened to, Mileva started thinking in a different way about life. Titel was the town where she comprehended the vastness of infinity, somehow entangled with the energy of the nature, and realized that her future should be school and dedication to reading books.

"Music and singing will be my leisure and satisfaction," Mileva used to say. "I don't want music to be my future profession."

Milos Marić then got her high school degree and in 1886 enrolled her in the first class of the Serbian Higher Girls School in Novi Sad.

There were twenty pupils in her class. A friend of hers, Jelisaveta Branko, went to the same class with her, and she would tell Mileva about it afterwards.

"She knew all the answers. She had always been quiet, reserved, and didn't want to attract the attention of the teachers. When she knew the answer, she would not raise her hand. We called her the 'saint'."

The Serbian school for girls, which Mileva attended, was in the building of the present-day restaurant called Staro Zdanje, just across the Matica Serpska. There were fourteen subjects at school, and she had excellent grades in all of them. Her class teacher was Mita Kalic. He taught Serbian and Hungarian.

Aleksandar Jorgovic taught her mathematics, and he was also talented in music. She resided with a widow, Katarina Polzovic.

The reason for her attending school in Novi Sad, which was in the vicinity of Titel and Kac, was because her mother was staying at her birth house with her relatives, together with Zorka and little Milos.

Novi Sad was a nice city. As early as 1790, a bookshop had been opened there that belonged to the metropolitan Stefan Stratimirovic, whilst during Mileva's schooling it belonged to a friend of her father's, Lazar Dundjerski. She could borrow a book from the library and expand her knowledge.

The next year, Mileva enrolled in the Realka High School in Sremska, Mitrovica.

The Marić family moved to Mitrovica in 1887. It was not recorded in the part of the town in which they lived.

Mitrovica had five thousand inhabitants at that time, and in 1881 it gained the status of a town. The foundations of the high school teaching in Mitrovica High School had been set in 1781 at the conference in Bjelovar, when the curriculum for a Slavic-German school was established. In the eighteenth century, Mitrovica had several schools: "The First German Trivial School," "The Second German Trivial School," and "The Girls' School and The Mathematics School."

In the document of the 22nd of April of 1784, it was recorded that there was "The Higher School of the Krajiska Headquarters," which later changed its name to the "Higher Headquarters School of the Krajiska Headquarters at the Petrovaradin-Slavic Area." It consisted of two trivial grades, and the third grade was called the "Oberschule." That third grade was the beginning of the third "Realka" High School, whereas the foundations of the Mitrovica mathematics lower "Realka" School, but it was only in 1838 that the foundations of a Lower "Realka" School which, since then, existed as the lower secondary school. Since 1863, in the schools of Mitrovica, religious instruction was taught at schools in the mother tongue, whilst in the high school in Mitrovica, history was taught as well. It was the period when mother tongue and German were equally taught at schools.

In that period, the general high school became the independent secondary school, and it had much more mathematics than some other high school. There were barely one hundred pupils, so each teacher could teach only nine pupils. It provided very good quality of education. The high school was very well equipped. It had a physics and chemistry laboratory with the collection of 1093 apparatuses, which proved that Mileva got the best scientific foundations in mathematics and physics just in that school. The teachers and professors were strict towards pupils, whereas the supervisors were even stricter and harsher towards teachers. Mileva enrolled in the second grade of the Lower General High School in the school year 1887–1888 upon passing the entrance examinations. It was the year when Lower Secondary School in Mitrovica transformed into the four-grade high school, which had the general educational character. The obligatory subjects were religious instruction, German, geography, history, mathematics, geometry, geometry drawing, physics, chemistry, and drawing in hand. In the first two grades, Mileva studied the principles of nice handwriting.

In the fourth grade of Mitrovica's high school, the subjects were the following: religious instruction, mother tongue, German, geography, history, mathematics, geometry and geometry drawing, physics, chemistry, and drawing in hand. Optional subjects were French, stenography, and gymnastics.

In this high school, Mileva showed her original ambitions in studying mathematics and physics, announcing special talent. She could use her imagination well, creating a clear picture of the text that she would be reading, showing deep concentration, which sometimes gave away the impression that the young girl was absent. Her profound thoughts showed her the mental picture that was so clear, almost real. Her ambitions grew together with the advancement of her knowledge. She could draw in a nice way, which could be seen on the original picture with the signature of her teacher.

The teacher of geography and history of Mila Maglic was the school, the manager of the Lower Secondary School. The pupils were studying foreign language using the dictionary of Dimitrije Isajilovic (1783–1853), who made up this dictionary of French, German, and Latin.

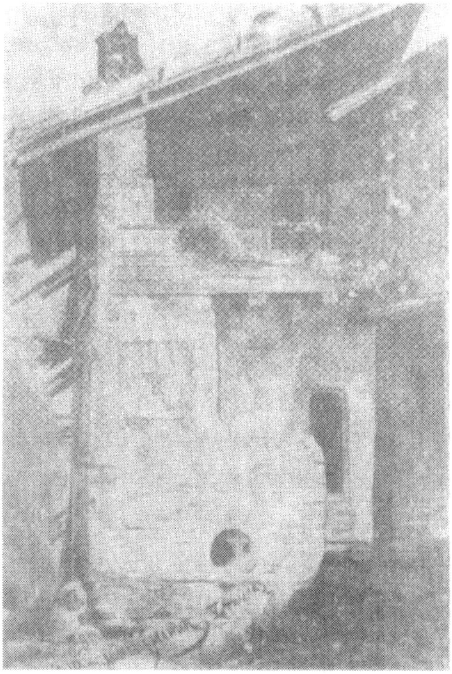

Figure 4: The original drawing of Mileva Marić

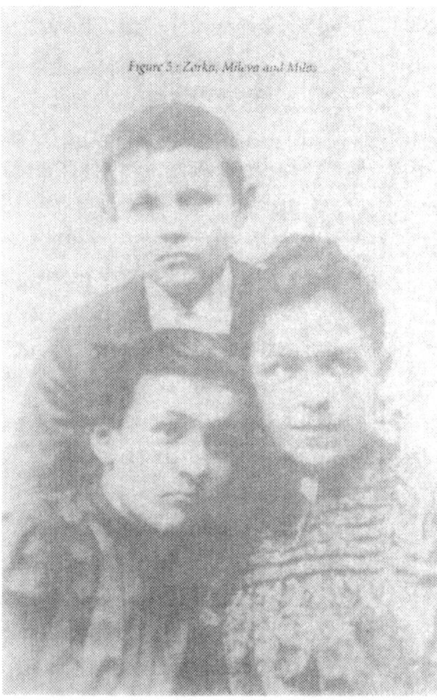

Figure 5: Zorka, Mileva, and Milos

Mileva's favourite book was *First Serbian Mathematics,* written by Vasilije Damnjanovic (1734–1792).

However, she showed interest in all kinds of books that were available because the town had at that time a Serbian town library and reading room, built in 1866. It was here that she experienced the magic moment of linking the military discipline and the strictness with scientific ambitions. She found all these in studying the life of the genius warrior Alexander the Great, who was her teenage idol. She admired that glorious warrior who had lived in the fourth century before Christ who, in conquering Persia, apart from the soldiers, had taken numerous scientists and soldiers along. This great warrior had been fond of scientific research and medicine. He wrote to Aristotle: "I would rather be proud of the most exciting knowledge than of this governing. Knowledge is what each man should search for."

Mileva was impressed by these words of Alexander the Great, and she would remember them throughout her life.

After she had finished Lower Secondary School in Mitrovica, Mileva went to Sabac. She showed, according to her sister Draga's words, great interest in learning. She was bright, with a particular affinity for mathematics. When she would be resting from studying, she would not play like other children did, but she would make up the tasks for herself and try to solve them. The teachers in the school in Sabac were amazed, and they told Milos Marić that his daughter Mileva would become famous and distinguished in her profession due to mathematics. She finished the fifth grade of high school in Sabac with excellent grades. However, she did not finish the sixth glade in Sabac because her father got a work transfer to Zagreb. The whole family worried how they would manage in that unknown city. On the other hand, Marić praised Zagreb as a beautiful and modern European city. His father used to talk about Zagreb in 1839, telling them that it had high buildings, long cobbled streets, and four-horses carriages, in which the noblemen, dukes, and barons would drive, in the front the ornate driver, called "husars," would sit (soldiers, the horsemen).

"People from Slavonia and Vojvodina used to come to Zagreb at that time on their horse-drawn vehicles to the market," said her father, adding, "Our fishermen used to sell the dried fish, doormats, and paprika. They do it today just like they did it decades ago. Today, there are a number of inns and shops with fine European goods. The books were, my dear Mileva, written mostly in German, which does not bother you, I hope." In 1892 her father was transferred on a work post of an official of the KP of Ban's Government in Zagreb.

The whole family moved to Zagreb then, settling at number 72 at Potok. Mileva enrolled as a private pupil in the high school in Zagreb in the sixth grade again. She was allowed to listen to the teaching in physics and mathematics, which was rare for girls at that time. In September 1894, she passed the exams of the seventh grade with best marks from mathematics and physics. Her father, Milos, submitted an application to the Great High School to free her from taking the exam in Greek, which she had not learnt before. His application was refused, so Mileva had to study Greek. In the first semester, the genius Mileva showed great success in learning Greek from the famous philologist, the translator Koloman Rac. The high school in Zagreb had the great collection of physics instruments, which provided good foundations for exploring experimental physics.

In the year 1895, the Marić family moved to Zurich, Switzerland. Zurich was the city at that time, with 150,000 inhabitants, with wide streets on which the horse-drawn trams would run, the horse-drawn vehicles, and other similar carriages. The city was built by the lake. Numerous boats reminded Mileva of Titel, her birthplace.

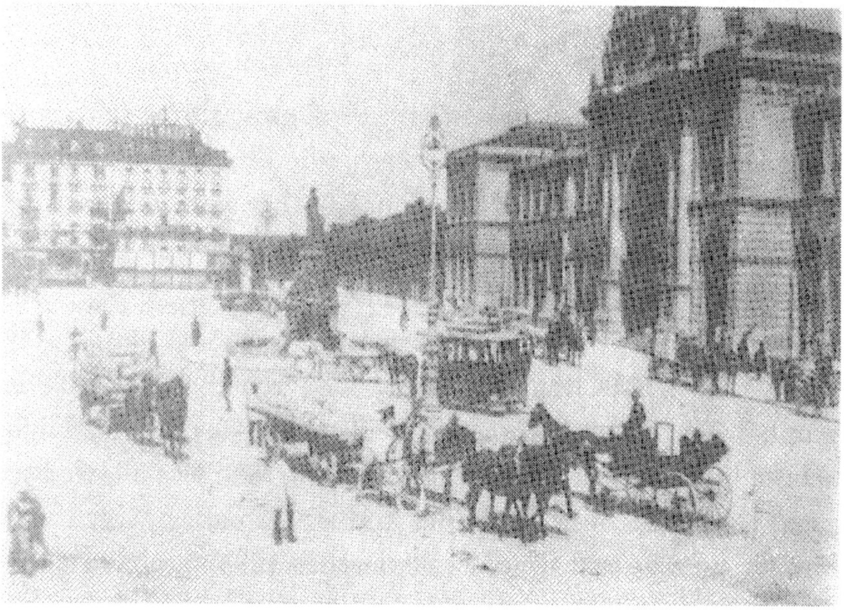

Figure 6: Zurich, 1896

Mileva attended the fourth semester grade as the expert student of the Higher Girls' School in Zurich. She listened to lectures of famous German novelist Rikarda Huh. It was the last grade of the secondary school, which she finished like all others with excellent grades. She passed the graduation exam in Federal Medicine School in Bern.

At that time, the girl already showed she had a high deductive mind and knew how to enter the sphere of the pure thought. She showed great interest in metaphysics, philosophy, and mathematics, but she was mostly enchanted with mathematics.

This versatile student wanted to enroll the studies of medicine upon finishing high school.

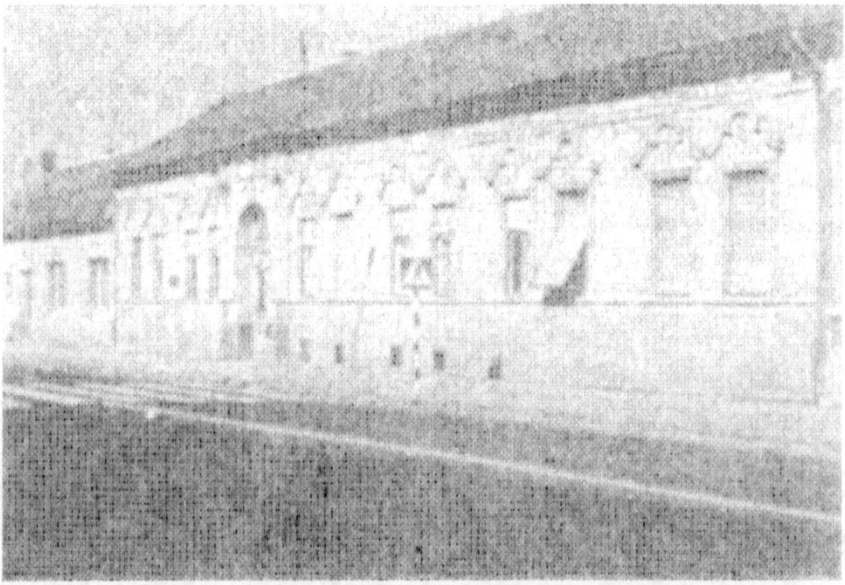

Figure 7: The family house of the Marićs in Novi Sad

She was probably under the influence of Augusta Bucek, a friend of hers, who lived in Zagreb, and who also studied medicine, but Mileva soon rejected those thoughts, realizing that mathematics and physics were her whole life.

From Zurich, Milos Marić decided to go back to Kac, to Novi Sad. In 1900 he moved to a house at number 20 on Kisacka Street.

On the foundations of the old house, Milos Marić built a new house in 1907, which exists even today. It is a two-number house due to its size and length. It was built in Baroque and Secession style, with twelve windows above which the women's figures stand, together with the palm's branches and with attic windows ornate with boy's masks protecting the house, with floral motifs. The house has a two-winged wooden door, "einfort" gate. In that house the Marić family would spend their winters, whilst in summer they would live in Kac and Titel.

Mileva stayed then in Zurich. It was the first time that she had separated from her family. Zurich would remain her new home, and she would be tied to it forever.

COSMIC CONTACTS OF MILEVA MARIC AND ALBERT EINSTEIN ENTWINED IN A NEW VISION OF THE WORLD

As long as there is breath in me
As long as there is strength in me
The essence of my being shall belong to you.
In the trail of the heavenly scientific truth
forever shall live just one name: the name of Einstein.

If our friendship depended on time and space, then we would, by overcoming time and space, ruin our brotherhood.
If we overcome space, what is left to us is just "here."
If we overcome time, what is left to us is just "now."

Don't you think that we shall meet from time to time
on this road between "now and here"?

(Taken from The Gull of Jonathan Livingstone, *by Richard Bach)*

In the Province of Vojvodina, in the south Austro-Hungarian monarchy, at the end of the eighteenth century, Serbs from the country formed bourgeoisie. It was the time when peasant jacket mingled with gentleman coat, peasant shoes with gentleman shoes, and patriarchal view of life with the philosophical one.

Our free bourgeois thought emerged under cruel and difficult circumstances. Serbian intellectual elite from Vojvodina used to go to Vienna, Budapest, Zurich, and Graz in order to study at the university. They all possessed the same traits: characteristic strong vitality striving towards progress, sane humanism, and philosophy of life. They wanted to increase their knowledge and make their views more progressive by going to a foreign world. They carried with themselves a positive view of life, and they were not afraid of the "big world." They also carried with themselves patriarchal principles of a Serbian family with a powerful tradition.

When Mileva decided to study polytechnics in Zurich, she immediately faced numerous refinements. One of the refinements was the fact that she was the first woman to enter the Faculty of Polytechnics (Swiss Poly).

Mileva Marić, slightly hesitating, climbed up the marble stairs towards the building of Federal Polytechnikum in Zurich, which was one of the most famous research and scientific centers in Europe. That very day, fate decided that Mileva would become a student of this faculty and change her life forever.

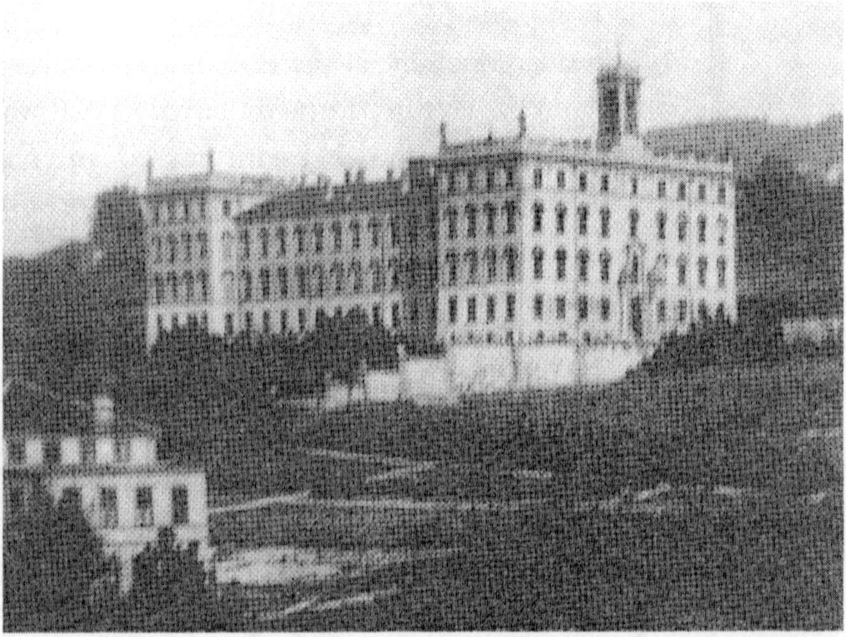

Picture 8: The building of the Faculty of Polytechnics in Zurich, 1905.

Uncertainty and fear filled her soul while standing in front of the huge building of the Faculty of Polytechnics, which was becoming ever bigger each instant. *How I wish this long waiting terminated,* she thought. *Are they going to say, "Miss, you do not belong here"*? Mileva abhorred such a thought and felt some indefinable movement and rage inside her. Words of her father, a dignified and distinguished gentleman from Vojvodina, ran through her mind.

"Do not enter the battle if you know in advance that you will lose. Fear is your greatest enemy. Do not forget, only you can decide where you belong. Only those who know what they want can be successful; thus, do not avert your eyes from the goal, and forget about all impediments. In life, a battle can be lost, but war can always be won."

As she was thinking about these words, Mileva mustered courage and grinned. Her father would always explain everything using military tactics.

In a moment, Mileva realized that her father's words became her loadstar, her inner strength, a vow that converted her greatest fear into the energy of success. She had been uncertain until that significant moment whether she should enter the faculty or abandon this idea forever.

Later on, she spoke about this moment of hesitation. "Suddenly, I was bursting with energy after I had felt my father's words deep in myself. In that crucial moment, everything was at stake, both life and death. From that moment on, I became aware of each and every moment of my life. From then on, I was simply a great energy moving towards success, towards a definite goal."

Mileva entered the building of the Faculty of Polytechnics, resolute and self-confident, full of energy of success. She discovered in herself a pure scientific spirit and a resolution to purge herself from the fatal inferiority complex with the strength of her father's words. However, a trait of harshness and strictness, which characterized Šajkaš soldiers, would be her inherent distinguishing feature. She remained reserved, distrustful, and taciturn.

Today, her soul was taken by some strange curiosity, mixed with light and warm unrest, and her heart was looking forward to the success. She entered the hall of the building of the Faculty and patiently, along with other students, waited for the results of the entrance examinations.

Her regular education and the highest grades from mathematics and physics and all the praises for being a specially gifted student of a brilliant mind gave her the confirmation that she would certainly pass the entrance examination. However, no woman had ever become a student of Polytechnics so far. Mileva did not know whether, being a female, she would be accepted at such a university. The stream of her thoughts was interrupted by the assistant, who suddenly opened the door, went out of a lateral room and, dumbfounded, stood in front of Mileva. Dryly and confusedly, he murmured under his breath, "I thought it was a mistake." A few seconds after, he added, "Miss Marić, will you please follow me to the main laboratory to see Professor Weber?"

Mileva came in and stood near the professor's desk, at first not daring to make a move, but the energy of success was stronger than fear. She stepped into a new world and bravely approached the professor's desk. He did not notice her, still staring at her examination test that was graded with the highest grades.

Mileva introduced herself in a loud and firm voice. "Professor Weber, I am Mileva Marić."

Taken by surprise, Professor Weber looked at her and murmured, "Yes, miss?" obviously thinking that this young girl got lost.

"I am Mileva Marić. I took the entrance examination at your department."

The professor opened his eyes widely and spoke confoundedly. "For Christ's sake, do not you know, young miss, from where you have come? It is courageous, and I must admit, it makes you special. Do not you know that you are the first woman who dared enter the Faculty of Polytechnics? I suggest you had better go to some girls' school, where you belong. Here, dear miss, you need not just intelligence which, according to the excellent results from the entrance examination, I am certain you possess, but also strength, persistence, and courage."

The girl started to defend herself fiercely. "Please, Professor, do not judge what you see." Pointing at herself, she continued. "I accept every obligation, challenge, and learning. It is the meaning of my life. My wish is to gladden my curious heart with hard work and learning."

The professor retorted dryly, "If you, miss, can overcome all the difficulties you are, then accept and from this moment on, you will be the first woman to enter Polytechnics in Zurich."

Mileva listened to the professor's words with natural dignity, and she was quiet and determined in behavior. She thanked the professor reservedly, and in her chestnut-colored eyes, there was a sparkle of happiness, mixed with the fear for the future and some deep, mysterious shade, known only to her, that she had to follow.

Mileva started with her studies in October 1896. She entered the Federal Polytechnics in Zurich, the department of the sixth school for the specialists of mathematics, along with eleven freshmen. Students abbreviated the official name of the Faculty into Poly, and 841 students studied at the Faculty at that time. This Faculty educated future teachers of physics and mathematics.

After she had passed the entrance examination, she searched for an apartment. She found it in the house of Bechtold Jochen and tried to organize her own life without the support of her family, whom she missed so much.

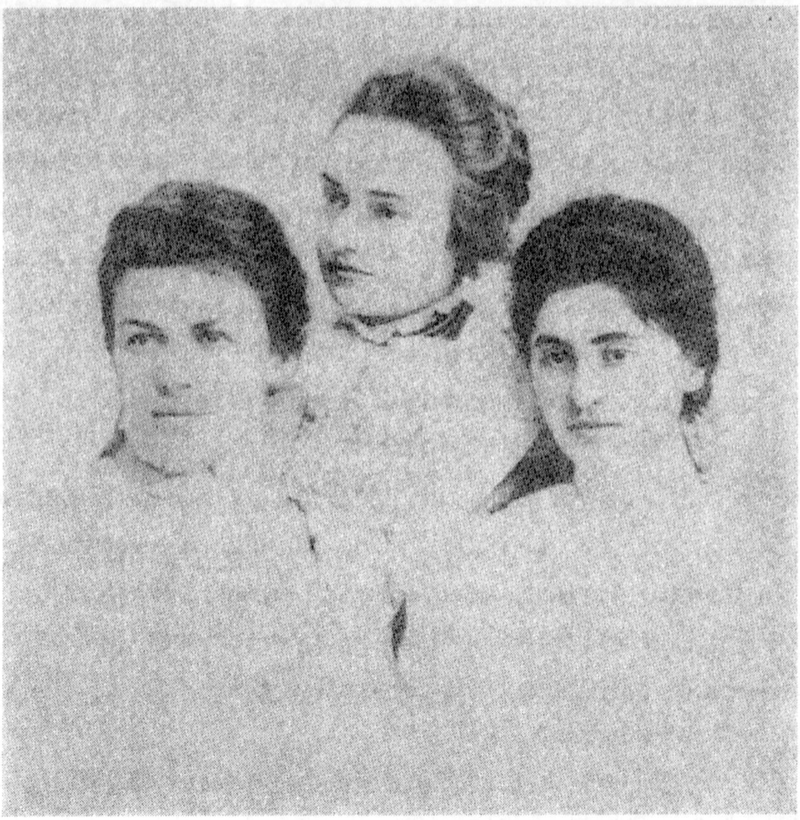

Picture 9: Mileva Marić (whose beauty is obvious) with her friends

Now she was completely devoted to her scientific research of physics and mathematics. In order to deepen her previous philosophical knowledge, acquired while spending her days in Ruma, Sremska, Mitrovica, and Kać, she signed up for the special philosophy courses. She attended them regularly, but what she had always been especially interested in was mathematics. She was thirsty for knowledge and searched into everything that was in any way connected to mathematical problems and mathematical constructions. She solved the most complicated problems easily and quickly, without any effort. She was a hardworking student, and she attended every single lecture from mathematics and physics. Since she had obtained knowledge from these subjects acquired in grammar school, she wanted to deepen and bring them to perfection. At the lectures, Mileva simply absorbed higher mathematical laws, learning from the most prominent scientists of the time, like Adolf Hurwitz and Hermann Minkowski (a German mathematician and physicist). Some other, equally splendid mathematicians gave lectures on different parts of higher mathematics. In order to understand mathematics, some previous knowledge was indispensable as well as hard work, of course, and a regular attendance of the lectures.

Soon after the admission, Mileva became friends with the student Grossman, who attended lectures from physics and mathematics, the compulsory subjects, with the same zeal as Mileva. Students exchanged thoughts and notes. Mileva demonstrated remarkable skills for concise representation of the subject matter, as she wrote her notes in a beautiful handwriting, typical for a girl.

Together with Mileva, the Faculty of Polytechnics entered the youngest student, Albert Einstein. However, he did not attend the lectures regularly, because he used to say that he had nothing to learn there, that there were no innovations and no movements. His main critics were directed towards Professor Weber. In the Pernet's laboratory, Einstein did not conduct the experiments according to the instructions. He did them in his own way and, as his biographer Kuznjetzov said, gave himself the freedom to disrupt the codex even more, addressing Weber as "Mr. Weber" and not "Professor Weber."

Einstein was loose and happy, and he easily surmounted the difficulties of life; in fact, we could say he was happy because of his own decision. In the morning, when he would get up, he had a choice: happiness or sadness. The young student always chose happiness, carrying the inner drama in his soul, hidden from the eyes of the world.

He had millions of opposite ideas, and he was profoundly dissatisfied, above all, with the rules of stiff professors who were supposed to teach him physics and mathematics. Moreover, he was dissatisfied with himself because his life was not going in the wanted direction. Ideas simply flowed in his thoughts, and the young student was severely tempted because he did not know how to adjust to them and it confused him. He tried to connect logically all he felt in himself by combining new elements of concepts and words. His intention was to create his own physical reality. However, his thought was not clear and productive. For all that he wanted to achieve, the knowledge of many words, symbols, different mathematical branches, rules, and ways of calculations was essential.

Main elements of his thinking were visual comparisons and a philosophical stand. He regularly attended additional classes from history and philosophy, and it gave him a great pleasure. At these additional classes from philosophy, he got to know better his older colleague, Mileva Marić, whom he first met at the laboratory.

He realized she had a profound thought when she participated in the discussions, although she participated quite rarely. She could comprehend clearly both physical and logical reality in cosmic world, saying, "It is all outside ourselves, the entire nature and cosmos; it is all part of ourselves, interweaving into a whole unit called the soul of the world."

Her mind and the depth of her spirit enabled her to draw an exact conclusion without any additional assumptions, which made her specially gifted. A law that could be confirmed by an experiment was above everything else to her. A young student of Jewish origin, Einstein was ready to dispute, to compare everything, and to view the world around him critically, sometimes even the knowledge of his older colleague, Mileva. Each day they were closer and closer, since Einstein wanted Mileva to search certain areas of theoretical physics together with him. He was not particularly interested in mathematics. Afterward, when he had already become famous, Einstein spoke about mathematics. "I saw," he wrote, "that mathematics is divided into numerous special areas and that each of them can occupy the whole short life that is given to us. I also saw myself in the position of Buridan's ass that cannot decide which haystack to take. Evidently; the problem was in the fact that my intuition in mathematics was not strong enough to differentiate clearly between what is essential and important from the rest, unnecessary, knowledge. Apart from that, the interest in the investigation of the nature was, doubtlessly stronger; I, as a student, had not yet understood that the access to the deepest principle problems in physics required the finest mathematical methods."

One day, after the additional philosophy classes, jokingly, Albert Einstein suggested to Mileva that she should give him protection. "Life is full of dangerous beasts, and you, miss, you are one of the most wonderful women I know." While saying this, he gently took her by her hand. Mileva, although almost four years his senior, was not ready for these unusual words of her colleague, and she was almost embarrassed.

Albert had already had certain love experience by that time. He knew how to entertain women's hearts with his jokes; he spoke wonderful, warm words; and he possessed certain strange, natural gentleness that would open the doors of women's hearts. Until this encounter with Mileva, he had had various girlfriends whom he had forgotten a long time ago. His heart had already been filled, for the first time, with true love for Maria Winteller. He called her "my dear, gold, sweet little angel." She was his professor's daughter, a professor whom he specially admired and respected.

Albert was staying at the professor's home while attending the fourth grade of secondary school in Arau. His sweet Maritza was nineteen, and he was seventeen. It was a real platonic love, but it was forgotten as soon as Albert had moved to Zurich. From then on, his only wish was to become a professor of theoretical physics. Biographer Armin Herman stated that Einstein escaped from this love, as he himself said, "to the high palace of the peace of soul," because he did not want to free his feelings. Nevertheless, a long time after the break-up with her, he sent her his dirty laundry to wash. When his younger sister Maya married Winteller's younger son, the Wintellers became his friends.

Albert's first flattering words asking from Mileva to give him her protection, Mileva discarded, saying, "A devil." She knew about his relationship from Arau, and he also spoke to her about his little Maria. "As soon as I look at her, I turn crazy again," he used to say. Mileva's patriarchal upbringing, inherent uncommunicativeness, and self-containment, as well as her longtime wish to meet true love, and former Albert's relationship from younger days—all of these represented true impediment, an obstacle to accept any courting of her younger colleague.

However, it was not what destiny meant for her. It is true, we ourselves cannot order our hearts whom they should love, and whom they should not. He kept courting Mileva in an easygoing manner, saying nice, pleasant words, and sometimes he would lightly touch her with his hand or a lock. His attention made Mileva feel nice, but her sense kept telling her that she should not let this love flourish. She remembered how she singled out the young Jew of German origin, Albert Einstein, among all the students, as soon as they had started studying. He had strange warm eyes and a gentle radiant face, which made him different from the others.

While practicing at the Institute for physics, he approached her cordially, directly, and jokingly. "Miss, I have been watching you for several days, and I have noticed grief and significant changes on your face. I am afraid that the studies or Zurich may not do you good. On the other hand, I saw you produce the results of experiments handily and with ease. Thus, I am curious to know how you achieve such a concentration and a quick solution, handling at the same time the grief which reads from your eyes."

"I appreciate your worry, Mister," Mileva replied reservedly and halted, realizing she did not know his name.

He smiled and put out his hand, a hand that simply implored to be taken. "My name is Albert Einstein."

For some moments, the girl hesitated, and eventually, she took his hand. "I am Mileva Marić."

It was the moment when a great friendship began, as well as a strange kind of respect and appreciation between these two young people. Einstein used to point out the values of his colleague Mileva frequently. She disliked praises, defending herself humbly from them, but Albert kept praising her, persuading her at the same time, half-jokingly, "If you want to be my friend, you have to learn to accept my praises and to understand my heart, which admires your intellect."

At that very moment, some strange, invisible bridge of mutual understanding was made, along with some mysterious common thread. From that moment on, Mileva simply had had him under her skin; he had become her habit and a part of her being, although she did not want it at all. Soon, she realized that the cheerfulness, warmness, even the simple talk, scientific discussions, and that special vivacity of Albert attracted her to him as a magnet.

His roguish, jolly face flickered in the eyes of Mileva Marić. A wonderful, pure feeling of love would come over her entire being, and she resisted with a great difficulty. The only solution she had was to conceal that new feeling deep in her heart. However, young Einstein showed each day more openly that he was in love with his older colleague. She also sensed that he cherished her, and that he wanted her and her knowledge from mathematics and physics. Each further encounter of the two was not only beautiful and warm, but it became a kind of hunger. It became passion mixed with love and some strange inner ardor to which this loving couple had to surrender.

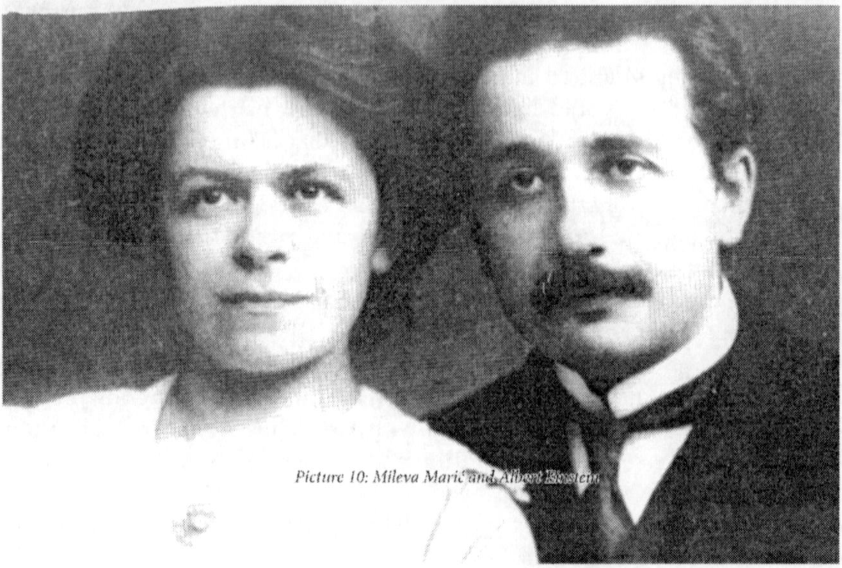

Picture 10: Mileva Marić and Albert Einstein

During their first date, they did not sense that their paths were predestined by a common fate of scientific work and research. The love they felt was a cosmic plan. Albert did not even suppose that in a cold, taciturn girl he would discover a passionate, loving, faithful, and marvelous woman. She was a woman ready to give herself for love, and their relationship even then became unusual, extraterrestrial, sensual and, above all, beyond the usual life. Everything between them was unified in a single level of destiny, without a clear line, which many of Mileva's and Albert's biographers tend to make.

However, Mileva's cold logic and rationality disapproved of this love, which was borne so suddenly. As soon as the holiday had begun, after the end of the winter semester, in 1896–1897, Mileva went to Kać and Titel to cure her wounded heart. She wanted to try to forget her secret, passionate love towards young Einstein. "Distance and time will be my alies," Mileva consoled her wounded heart. Far from Zurich, Mileva spent her days at the banks of the rivers Tisa and Danube, enjoying warm air and wonderful nature. She took upon herself a new task. *I shall give in to my emotions. I cannot permit myself to be like dry soil depending on a drop of rain. I cannot permit him to become the master of my heart,* Mileva thought, and made a decision to forget about it all.

It was as if Einstein knew some ancient secret, some magic formula of love, which Mileva just could not resist. "I just have to collect my thoughts and I shall forget him easily," Mileva consoled herself. However, his face flickered in her eyes, surrounding her. He was in every flower, in a mist wandering the fields; he was concealed in a stray white cloud.

Days passed. She was supposed to go back to Zurich, and her love wounds had not entirely healed. However, there, in Kać and Titel, she found peace and tranquility, and she turned to her only love: science. Then, for a moment, she halted on the way of pure scientific learning and listened to the whispers of mysterious words in the depth of her soul, the words that were born as witnesses of vanished epochs.

It was the moment when the luster of cosmic expanses lay on her heart and gave it strength and the energy of an explorer who wanted to step into the universe.

Young student Mileva, in contact with the universe, remembered her first version of the Milky Way and also the branches of a big tree. She remembered her earlier contemplations on the eternity of soul and world, and she realized how lonely and barren, as a rock, her life had been so far. It was a contentless, empty life, filled with fear and doubts. She realized she should lead the way of scientific research. Clearer than ever, she recalled the words of Josif Pančić, the words learned a long time ago, which she knew even then by heart. This is how he defined scientific principles of criticism,: "Critic is the most brilliant occurrence in our scientific progress...We analyze again the hypotheses which world have deeply respected for centuries, we abandon truths which seemed absolute until recently, and we grasp secrets, those secrets that have been beyond human mind."

She felt as if she had known all of it because it was written in her subconsciousness. "Spiritual masters" who imposed strict rules upon the world were erased from her mind, and she did not have any authorities anymore. Mileva opened the doors of her subconsciousness to the free thought that lives in the eternal time. For the first time, she felt freedom that enabled her travel to cosmos, using her thoughts only. Confinements in front of her were destroyed in a moment and had no power over her. Even the unpleasant defect, the ill leg, was not an obstacle for a steady step into a new sphere of life. Her goal was clear-cut, with the shape of future and with the brilliant scientific mind gazing at the cosmic distances. She contemplated, "Can one talk about the categories of time and space, without the restrictions of human thought? If we could just step into the universe, the picture of the world would be completely different. Only then would men understand the divine essence and the strength of light."

There, in Kać, she underwent the radical change of her own personality and mentality. There, in the starry sky, she became aware of the universal wisdom, making a strong decision of her life: From then on, only a scientific thought would have the access to her heart. No man would be in her heart again. That heart of hers would become the oasis of scientific peace. From then on, she was gifted with the venturous spirit, unusual courage, and self-denying work. Desanka Trbuhović said about her, "She is a woman of the southern tradition."

For simple people, Mileva's life was a strange model of living, in which everybody felt uncomfortable and ill at ease. She lived only for her work. The limits of her life, no man could envisage at that time. Although it was impossible to tell the limits of her existence, one sentence can explain it all: "She lived as she did, because she was chosen."

Mileva decided she would continue her studies in Heidelberg. On October 5, 1897, she left the Polytechnics in Zurich, and she spent her winter semester in Heidelberg.

In that new social environment, she dedicated herself to science and nature, trying to reach for the distant worlds. Love that she felt for Einstein and those beautiful feelings for Zurich were profoundly suppressed. Mileva thought they were dead forever. It can be understood from the letter she sent to Albert Einstein from Heidelberg, in which pure friendship and restraint dominated, "It has been quite a long time since I received your letter, and I would like to respond to it, to express my gratitude for your sacrifice, as you wrote four long pages. I would also like to thank you for the happiness you gave me on one picnic, although once you told me to write to you only when I have nothing to do. I am, nevertheless, rather obedient (just ask Miss Bethold), and I just waited for this feeling of boredom to come over me. However, this waiting has been futile until today, and now I just do not know what to do. It seems that I would have to wait until the Judgment day, and, hence, you could justly think of me as of a barbarian. On the other hand, if I decide to write to you, then it will not be in accordance with my consciousness.

"I am now, as you have already heard, living among German oaks, in the lovely Neckar Valley. Unfortunately, the beauty of the valley is covered with the dense layers of fog, and, however hard I try to see something, I can only catch glimpses of something indefinite, lonely and grey as infinity.

"I do not really think that the content of our cranium is to be blamed for human incapacity to comprehend the infinity. A human being could comprehend the infinity, only if a small man, as a young individual who learns to comprehend, would not be so strictly tied to a land, or even a nest, and if a man were not closed between the walls, but let to wander a little through universe.

"A man can easily imagine an infinite happiness, thus man should comprehend the infinity of space, as well, and I even think it could be a lot easier. People are so intelligent, they have achieved so much, and I can confirm it now with Heidelberg professors...."

Here, in Heidelberg, Mileva was obsessed with sublime thoughts, and she put before herself marvelous goals of scientific truth, which absorbed her whole being.

Near the end of the winter semester, she decided to return to Zurich. It may have been the moment when the finger of destiny set the path of Mileva Marić, and she fulfilled the mission given to her, the one because of which she came to this world. Albert Einstein was extremely glad to have her back.

Respected Miss,

...I am so glad about your intention to continue your studies here. Do it as soon as possible. You will not repent your decision. I am convinced that in a short span of time, you will make up for all the important lectures we have had so far...

Albert Einstein

Albert was looking forward to her return and named her "a little runaway."

After she had returned from Heidelberg, Mileva took a restrained and a friendly stand towards Albert, but they kept company, a reserved and a slightly cold one. They exchanged books and notebooks, spent their time together, and frequently talked about their common books, research, and interests. Mileva worked hard to compensate her absence from Zurich studies, devoting all her efforts to terminate the summer semester successfully.

Being near her love again, however hard she tried to stay cold and restrained, a spark of love and adoration flared in her. Admittedly, this spark was encouraged by Albert's beautiful love words. The old company from Zurich was together again, like the old times. Mileva played the piano at their parties, and sometimes she would bring a "tamburica" and sing songs from Vojvodina with great pleasure. She could sing nicely, and her younger colleague Albert accompanied her, playing the violin.

Soon Mileva realized that she loved him even stronger than at the time when she went home on her summer holiday. The two were passionately in love, and they realized soon that they had much in common: the same scientific interest, the same studies, and this great love. When Albert went on his summer holiday, he wrote to Mileva.

Mileva was looking forward to his letters. She was in love, and she dreamed about his presence. She praised her beloved all the time; she told her parents about him, about his intelligence, cheerfulness, and greatness. "He is wonderful, warm-hearted; he can talk nicely, and he is my genius," she used to say. For days, she would retell her friends from Novi Sad Albert's sayings and his wisecracks.

It was the time when the shattered pieces of cosmic love were born peacefully in weak light, woven into the universal thoughts of a wistful love of the two young. Mileva retained certain restraint in her letters because she expressed her profoundest thoughts about different research. Hence, the letters seemed slightly cold. Nevertheless, these letters concealed sweet, wistful love.

Dear Mr. Einstein,

Your letters always provoke such pleasant feelings in me. On the basis of numerous experiences we have had together so far, totally inconspicuously, some special feeling has developed. It is aroused at the slightest touch, not necessarily awakening some detailed memories, and each time it feels like I am in my room again.

Mileva did not have courage to let her feelings be. She was afraid that the letters would come to Mrs. Einstein's hands, to his mother's hands and, hence, in the same letter, she said, "You, for certain, do not let anybody read my letters, do you? You have to promise me that. Once you said that you disliked everything that was simple; well, then, if this seems simple to me, do it for my love! What do you think?..."

Concealed love in Mileva's letters was comprehensible to her beloved Albert only. He knew that this silence was precisely a bridge of wistful wishes so well known to him. At the beginning of August 1899, he sent her a letter calling her his little doll, saying he could not understand she was not by his side..."The work we do together seems to me quite pleasant, good, beneficial, and above all, less monotonous...My mother and my sister are, as it seems to me, slightly narrow minded and philistine, no matter how much I am fond of them. It is strange how a way of life can change us, especially mentally, and hence, the closest family relations start turning into a friendship out of a habit. In the depth of our souls, we become so incomprehensible to each other that we cannot feel what the other one experiences and goes through..."

Love and science connected these two young people, who used to say, "We came into being at the common level of scientific research of integral particles in motion." These two beings were filled with the joy of love; Albert cherished her presence, and she was simply ill when he was not by her side. Their research in the area of mathematics and physics was substantiated by a new research, which was interrupted for a moment. These two young human beings were deeply in passionate love. They shared the same thoughts; they wanted to merge and do the scientific research together. It was the moment when two important links between the two people were created, and these were love and science. Albert was exalted about music and he played violin, whereas Mileva had a gift for music and she played the piano and could sing nicely. Einstein appreciated it a lot. Correspondence between Albert and Mileva showed that they lived together, although they still had separate apartments.

In nature, everything has its rhythm and order, its proportions and relations, and the two young people, Mileva Marić and Albert Einstein, formed part of that nature. They realized that there existed the wheel of being and that everything dies and flourishes again, living in eternity forever. Their goal was to reach the scientific essence and not to lose the path, although full of uncertainties. They set off together, gazing at a far visible line that extended to the infinity of cosmos. These two beings might have recognized each other for a moment, expressing supernatural sensibility. They might have had preserved deep in their subconsciousness a cosmic memory of soul and a memory of living together.

They had an unyielding interest that carried certain intentions and a goal that was to become a symbol of scientific achievement at the beginning of twentieth century. It was to become a symbol of humankind. A new theory that would make Einstein's name famous…

During the whole of the scientific research, Mileva and Albert were each other's mental ground from which they were created common universal concept of the world. Psychological cosmos was manifested through common work and through light threads that spoke in a spiritual tongue through these two scientists. Their minds were connected at higher levels of consciousness, interweaving in timeless, infinite dimensions through the world of psyche. They directed their energies to scientific research. Sensory information entered into the consciousness of two minds, creating with both of them scientific-reflective pictures of new psychological reality. All of these indicated predestination for these two people to be a higher cosmic choice. That is why we can claim justly that they were not related at conscious level of perception only. Their relation had a cosmic dimension, and this relation created the relativity theory. There is no doubt, the two young people in love mixed science and mystery. Cosmos opened before their eyes, a mysterious universe replenished with true wealth. This very universe was a treasury of memories that represented a recollection on past lives, and it enabled them to create the greatest scientific miracle, concealed from the eyes of a simple man until then. Einstein was (as his biographer said) allowed to dream and to think, to write discussions, to change the face of science, but Mileva Marić was the basis, the fundament, and the source of scientific cognition. Their "fields" were brought together and they functioned under common name: Einstein. Out of all of that emerged the inner dramatization that brought one thought—purification shown to the world—as a scientific, democratic, and warm human thought of unity.

That is how the name Einstein became a strange symbiosis of two beings liberated from every other pleasure, living in the inner common existence.

Their ideas followed in continuation until they became one theory, a theory magnificent to the whole world, and that was the relativity theory.

Albert and Mileva conveyed each other their ideas, communicating through their souls, crossing thus the line of thought and equalizing their minds. Mileva diminished her being and her identity for this generous love. On the level of the unconscious, because of her patriarchal upbringing, she gave preference to her future husband, who used her energetic constitution and came to scientific cognition that marked his world fame. Mileva had only her love for her beloved Albert Einstein, the love that was the only value in her life.

Many biographers of Albert Einstein who, admittedly, appeared decades after his death, tried to separate scientific thought or the very idea of relativity theory or quantum theory from genial mathematical work of Mileva Marić. Moreover, they denied not just her scientific contribution, but also her beauty, describing her as ugly, evil, grumpy woman, which is highly reprehensible.

However, what is certain is that this magnificent woman left eternal marks of her soul in cosmos, and that she flickered in the heavens like a comet, light of which lasted an instance and then turned into darkness forever. Mileva's soul had to fight against invisible evil forces that crossed her way as a scientist and as a woman. Love and science connected her with Einstein, to whom she dedicated herself. He succeeded in graduating at the Faculty of Polytechnics. Only five students took the graduation examination: Luis Kolnos, Marsel Grossman, Jakob Erat, Albert Einstein, and Mileva Marić. Albert was twenty-two years old, the youngest of all of them. Of these five candidates, Mileva's and Einstein's average grades were approximately 4 and 4.91 respectively.

Desanka Đurić-Trbuhović, Mileva's biographer, wrote about her: "During the whole of her studies, she achieved the greatest recognition and the highest grades. After Marsel Grossman, who was the first and certainly the best, Mileva had the second-best grades. Her final average grade at the end of her studies was 4.66, and Albert's was 4.59." He continued to live in Zurich, and there he completed his doctoral thesis. He could not find job, and he was disappointed, hungry, sloppy, without hope, but his Mitza was there for him to love him and support him materially and morally.

A fully devoted traditional Serbian girl fought for him, accepting all his troubles as his own. When Albert took his doctor's degree on June 1, 1901, he went to Winterthur, and Mileva tried to convince Professor Weber to accept Albert as his assistant. Revolted for not being able to change the professor's opinion, she abandoned her extensive doctor's thesis, which was excellent, and thus, she withdrew from her research studies. Devoting herself to her love, she denied herself. All attempts to find Albert a job were in vain. Mileva did not succeed in graduating because, even then, she started to sacrifice for her love openly, and her education suffered the consequences.

She passed the final examination the following year, but she did not get her diploma; women were not given diplomas. What she got was a certificate confirming that she finished the Polytechnics faculty.

At that time, she was already three months pregnant and that new situation confounded her even more. Einstein was not able to provide her a normal life, because he did not have a job. He tried to work as the assistant, then at least as a school teacher, but he did not manage either. Parents did not support him, because they did not accept his "sweet Mitza." His biographer, Armin, said, "And now, out of sheer commodity; as his parents interpreted it, by chance, he came across this Serbian student who tied him strongly to herself."

Mileva Marić was totally unlikable to Albert's mother, Paulina. Yet she spoke to her son in vain. "She is a book, as you are, but what you need is a woman. While you are thirty, she is an old witch."

Yet exactly in that woman, as they called her, "a book," Albert could read his prophecy for the future, and there he found the answers to his questions. She was a real temptation for him, and that was why he could not resist her. There he found a miraculous formula of life, which was about to change the world and make his wish for success come true. He conceived reality that connected him with both simple practical life and science.

All attempts to separate Albert from his beloved Mitza were without success. Albert loved her with true and tender love. He wrote to her, "Everybody but you are strangers to me." Mileva was more sensible than he was, and she tried to convince him to calm down, saying that everything was going to be settled. She tried to find different routes to the heart of Albert's mother, Paulina. "Have you spoken to her about me again? My dear, you have to endure so much for me." Albert Einstein responded, "My parents are, admittedly, worried because of my love towards you. Mama frequently sheds bitter tears, hence, I can say that I have not a single moment of peace here. My parents cry for me, as if I were dead. Again and again, they keep thinking that I shall disgrace myself if I tie myself to you. They think that you are not healthy...You cannot imagine how much I suffer...if only they knew you...They behave as if they were enchanted, and which is more, they think that I am the one who is enchanted...Love you with all my heart.

In young Albert Einstein, a poet who had fallen asleep a long time ago was awakened, and he was waiting eagerly his honey, while pacing in an empty room of an apartment for the single people.

However, Albert did not just wait for her because of love, but also because of the work they did together. "In Arau, a brilliant idea occurred to me, to search the impact of the relative movement of the body in relation to ether and the velocity of spreading of light in transmitters. Another theory crossed my mind, connected with that matter, and I find it quite possible..." Albert saw how her mysterious thought radiated mildness and friendliness. She took him to another world. She was always thoughtful and restrained, saying, "Every 'why' has its explanation."

Stable profoundness, born out of the sphere of subconciousness, was for her beloved Albert, with whom she had harmonious ideas and thoughts. With time, these became identical. Both of them felt love that interweaved with the scientific work. Mutual thread of the movement of the field of light would link the beings forever.

Mileva was content in Zurich with her beloved Johanzel (Johnny), but her happiness was gone as soon as she had found out that she was expecting a child. Albert soothed her, saying that everything was going to be just fine, that he would find a job and that they would get married then. She shuddered at the thought of confessing to her father that she would have an illegitimate child. She sat in her house for days, sad, with a grievous heart, sharing nothing with the others. She did not even spend time with her sister Zorka and her brother Mitoš. Zorka was a delicate girl, impetuous and restless, like a doe. She initiated the conversation with great joy, but sometimes she was rather odd. She laughed cheerfully and encouragingly, trying to ease the situation in which Mileva found herself.

At the end of the fall, 1901, Mileva's family received rather unpleasant letter from the Einstein family, which did not spare words and rebukes on Mileva's account. It only made even more difficult that new, unpleasant situation for Mileva Marić, who was expecting Albert's child.

She predominantly spent her days in Kać and Novi Sad, on Kisačka Street, expecting a letter from her beloved Albert.

It was a cold January in 1902. Mileva was nine months pregnant, spending her days in anticipation of her delivery, and most of the time she stared through frozen window glasses, shrouded in sharp layers of ice. The whole surroundings looked forsaken in this icy whiteness. Houses were covered with snow that reached even the windows. A small yellow puppy waded through the yard, and only his snout jutted out of the snow.

Suddenly, he barked cheerfully. That meant that somebody was arriving. A mailman with the big letter from Albert Einstein stood at the doorway. Mileva put on a leather cloak, passed through the hallway, and received the letter at the porch. Her mouth contorted a bit as if she was going to cry, and she looked at her mother, her eyes brimming with tears. Her mother, Marija, smiled and gave Mileva an encouraging look, accompanied with some short words: "Come on, cheer up, and do not worry. It will all be settled with time." Mileva shrugged her shoulders, did not say a word, and it meant she agreed. She believed her beloved. She knew he would never leave her or let her down.

My dear Mitzika,

Stay positive, my dear, do not let disturbing thoughts come to you. I shall not leave you and everything is going to be just fine. Just be patient. You will see, you will not feel bad in my arms, although it all might seem a bit stupid. How are you, my dear? What is the boy doing? It is going to be splendid when we get a chance to work together, and nobody will be able to interfere into our happiness. Then, your present worries will be compensated abundantly with a lot joy, and

our days will be passing peacefully, without unpleasant surprises...Do not be desperate, I shall do everything to take a good care of you, my dear.
Stay positive, and write as soon as possible a dear little letter to your
Jochanzel (Johnny)

During the last days of January, Mileva sighed quietly, and then she felt a strong pain in her belly that spread onto her back. A few hours later, she delivered a child named Lieserl. Mileva's heart was joyous. Everybody in the house accepted the newborn baby, and now they all expected a letter from Albert Einstein. The letter came soon.

"My darling...You see, Lieserl really came along, just as you wanted. Is she healthy and does she scream properly? How do her little eyes look? Who does she resemble more, you or me? Who feeds her with milk, is she hungry?...I love her so much, although I do not know her yet! Could you take a photograph of her, when you recover?..."

When Mileva recovered, and Lieserl was bigger, Albert called his dear Mitza, saying that he felt bad without her and that she should come under the auspices of his home. Mileva left Lieserl and went to Switzerland. The little girl fell ill from scarlet fever, and this illness damaged her heart a lot. Mr. Marić did not register the girl in the registry of births, expecting her parents to come soon to take the girl to Switzerland. In one letter (as the family claimed), Mr. Marić notified his son-in-law about little Lieserl's illness. He informed him that she was quite unwell and that her parents should take her to a doctor in Switzerland. Mileva was already expecting her second child, and apart from that, she worked hard on scientific research with Albert, who did not want anything to disturb their harmonious scientific work. After a couple of months, little Lieserl died, and Einstein again did not inform his wife. After a year, he admitted the truth, and Mileva never forgave him. It was the secret concealed by his married couple from the eyes of the contemporaries. Mileva bore the pain for the lost child all her life.

Albert searched for a job. He submitted applications wherever he could. Mileva advised him to try in Vienna and in Belgrade, but everything was in vain. Young people were desperate. Einstein wrote to Grossman: "It has been three weeks since I am staying with my parents in order to obtain the job of the assistant at a university. I would have had it a long time ago if Weber would not plot against me. Nevertheless, I do not waste any opportunity and I do not lose my sense for humor...God created a donkey and gave it a thick skin."

It was not until April 1902 that Grossman managed, with the help of his father, to get his friend Einstein a job at the department for patents in Bern. Only when Einstein got his job in Bern were the conditions established for him to marry Mileva.

Her soul was taken by some strange curiosity; it was a rapturous feeling of joy mixed with light, warm unrest, as if her heart anticipated a new world and a new hope from that day on. That was how Mileva Marić felt on that fateful day, on January 6, 1903, on Christmas Eve, when she married her beloved Albert Einstein.

It was noon when they married, exalted with each other, surrounded by their best friends. Not a single member of Albert's family attended the wedding. After a simple meal in a small restaurant, they went to their apartment at 49 Krom Street. As soon as they arrived, they realized that Albert had forgotten the key, which happened so frequently. We could say that this locked door represented a symbol of impediments to the future happiness of the newlyweds. It was the moment when two young beings initiated their life together, bringing to the marriage their personal traits only. Albert carried in himself a radical spite against the existing scientific laws and rules, and his ideas were always expressed through inner, concealed emotions, frequently transient.

Rational, intelligent, taciturn, and somehow strangely dignified, Mileva had had a book as a friend all her life. She carried in herself a systematic knowledge of mathematics and physics, a seed of creativity, a logical way of thinking inherited from her deep roots of spite. Mileva had a spark of freedom and profound intelligence, typical of the bourgeoisie of Vojvodina. She carried well-established, patriarchal rules about marriage, marital obligations, and eternal love. She was faithful to her beloved Albert all her life. High moral conscious of a Serbian wife and mother were the most honorable characteristic of hers. It could be justly said that the love and the research Albert and Mileva did together were not at a conscious level of perception. They lived in a broader inner reality, which was manifested in new ideas and new proves before the eyes of the world. Mileva represented a laboratory where future reality was to be born. Albert's ideas transformed into physical proof and regularity there.

She possessed natural inherent balance of senses and mind and a great gift to observe and highlight what was the most conscious and the essence of sensual, scientific research. She was a real master in analytical approach; she knew how to make a conclusion and how to separate important from unimportant. She never withdrew from her own thoughts, even less from the other people's thoughts.

Mileva respected her own expression of scientific thought, and she was frequently reserved and seemed cold and calm when facing lots of new observations. Before speaking, she would have judged her thought, and only than did she pass her judgment. Later on, biographers of Albert Einstein misused that reservedness to impair the value of her scientific contribution the relativity theory. They did not realize that Mileva first acknowledged bold critical observations with her consciousness, then turned them over to her subconsciousness and, eventually, proved and analyzed, they came to her beloved Albert. Their research and their discussions began with the oldest philosophical knowledge, which was introduced in 2,500 BC. They discussed in which positions individual objects are placed when related to one another, as well as their creation and movement of identical objects. One of the topics, interesting to both of them, was Aristotle. He was a popular and a frequent topic of discussions at the meetings of a group formed by Albert Einstein, who named it "Olympic Academy."

"Although it seemed that, by very thinking, correct results can be produced with respect to the observed objects, such a 'miracle' was based on mistakes. Yet, to those who experience such a miracle for the first time, miraculous seemed the fact that humans are capable of achieving such a degree of reliability and pureness in abstract thinking, as the Greeks showed us for the first time in geometry." (Kuznjetzov)

Mileva was rather happy in the first few years of her marriage with Albert. She worked with him on a new scientific research, and their work contributed to the strengthening of their love.

In cooperation with Paul Habicht, Mileva worked on a construction of influence machine for measurement of small electrical potential. By multiplication, when the machine was finished, Einstein took care of the protection of the patient and, naturally, the new invention was registered under the name Einstein-Habicht (patent number 35693).

It was the time when Mileva worked a lot, driving Albert to fall to work vigorously, but he did not like exhausting experiments and provings. He was always interested only in the final result. His ideas floated without bases sometimes, as a balloon, because they were not connected with the facts. Desanka Trbuhović said, "He loved to make her angry with his doubts in the correctness of her mathematical claims. However, Mileva stayed firm and, red in face, stamped her foot defending her work and her belief."

Einstein's mother, Paulina, and his aunt, as well as some of his friends, had prejudices about woman scientists, thinking it was a "result of pervertedness."

"Only out of change or out of an illness can a female develop other talents than those which enable her to love the better and to love maternity." (Armin Herman)

Einstein, however, called his Mitza a clever naughty because she was versatile: She could cook, make different kinds of cakes, sew, play instruments, sing nicely, and draw.

The Einsteins were rather happy. The first years of their marriage, spent in Bern, were especially happy and fruitful. Those were the years of new scientific inventions.

Theory of photoelectric effect, Mileva and Albert worked out together, in the period from 1904 to 1905.

The first woman of polytechnics remembered how she had had to prove herself at the faculty. Her knowledge always had to be brilliant, because "women did not belong there." She did not want to put her name on the scientific pieces of work she did with Albert, because the success of the work would have been denied. Mileva was not a fighter for women's rights. She just transferred willingly the fame to her husband.

Relativity theory is based upon experimental sources and mathematical proves. These are the means by which deducing of theoretical mathematics is done. "A lot of people believe that the relativity theory tells us that our universe is some kind of different world, 'Alice in Wonderland'; that mathematician Einstein discovered this as well as the fourth dimension, shortening and lengthening of objects, contraction and spreading of our world as if it was a balloon. In short, he discovered that everything is relative and mysterious (Leopold Infeld)."

Relativity theory between mass and energy was discovered in 1905, and it changed the face of science. It was the time when Einstein worked as an employee at the federal patent office in Bern. At that time, the greatest scientific pieces of work were created in the Einstein family, although Albert was rather young and inexperienced; as his biographers said, he was "a simple employee."

The Einsteins gave their contribution to the quant theory that was formulated in an article that appeared in 1905. The same year, it appeared in the booklet *Annalen der Phusik,* where the relativity theory was printed. Leopold Infelt said that only until 1905 can we follow the quant theory independently from the relativity theory. Interweaving of the quant theory and the relativity theory reflects in the atomic energy and its exploitation. Serbian biographer of Mileva Marić, Đorde Krstić, said that the famous formula $E = mc^2$ was born in Novi Sad.

It was summer 1905, and the Einsteins were pleased to have finished a great piece of work. They went to Novi Sad on a summer holiday. This is what Desanka Đurić-Trbuhović said about the Einsteins' visits to Novi Sad and Kać:

"World famous scientist Albert Einstein, and a man who married a girl from Novi Sad, had been there various times. First time it was with his wife, Mileva Marić, and their fourteen-month-old child. They visited her parents in summer

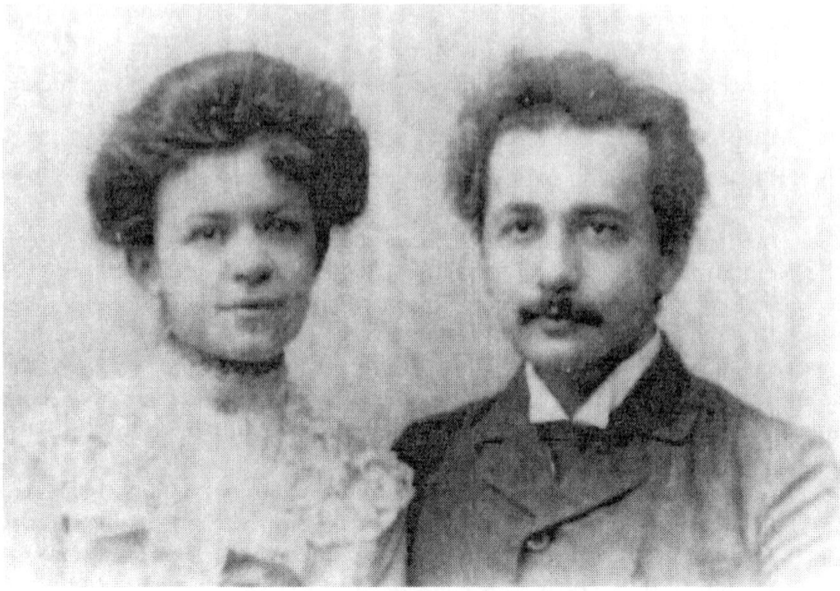

Picture 11: Mileva and Albert Einstein

1905 at the farm in Kać, where she had spent her childhood, and in Novi Sad on Kisačka Street."

The Einstein family was received ceremonially in the home of the Marić family. During the whole day, relatives and acquaintances came along to say hello to Mileva and her husband and son. Albert's behavior was natural and relaxed, and he carried his son on his back while walking across Novi Sad. The conversations were lively, and only Mileva's mother could not communicate with her son-in-law because she did not speak any foreign languages. Mileva (Mitza) was glad and satisfied that her family accepted Albert so heartily. At that point, she told her father, "We had just finished an important piece of work before we came here, and it is going to make my husband famous around the world!..." Albert himself said, during the conversation with highly educated gentlemen from Vojvodina, "I need my wife. She resolves all mathematical problems for me..."

The second time Einstein visited his in-laws was in 1907, and the same author said that Einstein was already an honored scientist.

Intellectual circles in the town of Novi Sad respected him greatly, but for them he was a weird man. He had untidy, long hair. Cheerful and smiling, he carried his son on his shoulders across the streets of Novi Sad. It provoked the petty bourgeois society that respected only conventional order and usual politeness. Albert deviated from this utterly, and that was why people used to call him "that crazy son-in-law of Marić."

Students gathered around his table at the tavern Erežbet Kiralina (Queen Elizabeth), where he liked to go. It is remembered that he said that he was not against a reasonable consummation of alcohol: "You see...I think that the Serbs are an ingenious nation. I judge this according to my wife." Later on, in 1933, Albert told Mihajlo Pupin in America, "Serbs are an able, gifted nation."

Intensive cooperation between the spouses, as well as their teamwork, lasted until 1911. The days from Bern were particularly successful and beautiful, and later on, Mileva and Albert recalled these days with wistfulness.

Mileva protected Einstein's interests in every field, supporting him, not only in his ideas, but in his actions as well. As a sign of rebellion, she withdrew her doctoral thesis from Dr Weber, because he allegedly hurt her beloved Albert.

On July 28, 1910, Mileva gave birth to her second son, Eduard, whom they affectionately called Tete. First matrimonial problems, we could say open conflicts, between Albert and Mileva, coincided with the moment they stopped working together in the field of science. When Albert Einstein became a full professor on April 1, 1911, Mileva found herself abandoned in Prague, at the margins of life. It was so difficult for her to adjust to the new social environment. Her younger son Eduard was eight months old, and the elder one, Hans Albert, was seven years old. Mileva started to withdraw into her "castle of silence and isolation"; she was moody and doleful. Albert, with his goings-out and his friends, became a stranger to her.

In Prague, Mileva suffered her decline as a woman. A hard work, which had lasted for years, left a mark on her face; she was no longer pretty; her big, dark brown eyes darkened. They reflected all the tiredness and pain that had accumulated for years. Although now they were rich and could afford servants, Mileva could not enjoy the commodities of a new life, because she realized she was losing what was the most precious to her: her husband.

In 1911, a congress was held in Brussels, attended by world-famous scientists of chemistry and physics, and Mileva Einstein was there as well. They say she used every opportunity to extol her husband and his scientific geniality, and not herself. However, in her contacts with the scientists her scientific profoundness, clear thoughts, and definite sentences did not pass unnoticed, and she impressed her collocutors. Mileva, however, did not want to magnify herself. She just fought wholeheartedly for her husband's return to Zurich, and he really did get the transfer rather soon. At the beginning of August 1912, the whole family moved to Zurich again. Mileva went on picnics with her children in the mountains; she enjoyed seeing her old friends and returning to Zurich, because it was her love from the period when she was a student. Switzerland became her second homeland. She expected that the return to Zurich would bring her the love and the harmony—in other words, the love of her husband. She dreamed of her estranged husband falling in love with her again. Mileva also dreamed of being included in her husband's scientific research, of working again with Albert, as it used to be.

However, the matrimonial crisis of the Einsteins affected all the segments of their lives, although the marriage still existed. In 1913, in Kać and Novi Sad, the Einsteins came in order to baptize their sons, Hans Albert and Eduard, in Orthodox St. Nicolas Church in Novi Sad.

Мали Швајцарци православне вере.

Јуче су у овдашњој српској православној алмашкој цркви крштена два мала Швајцарца, синови дра Алберта Ајнштајна, професора на свеучилишту у Цириху, а унуци нашег цењеног пријатеља и суграђанина Милоша Марића. Мали Алберт и Едуард крштени су у православној вери по жељи свога деде Милоша.

Morning issue of "Zastava," from Tuesday, September 23, 1913, no. 202

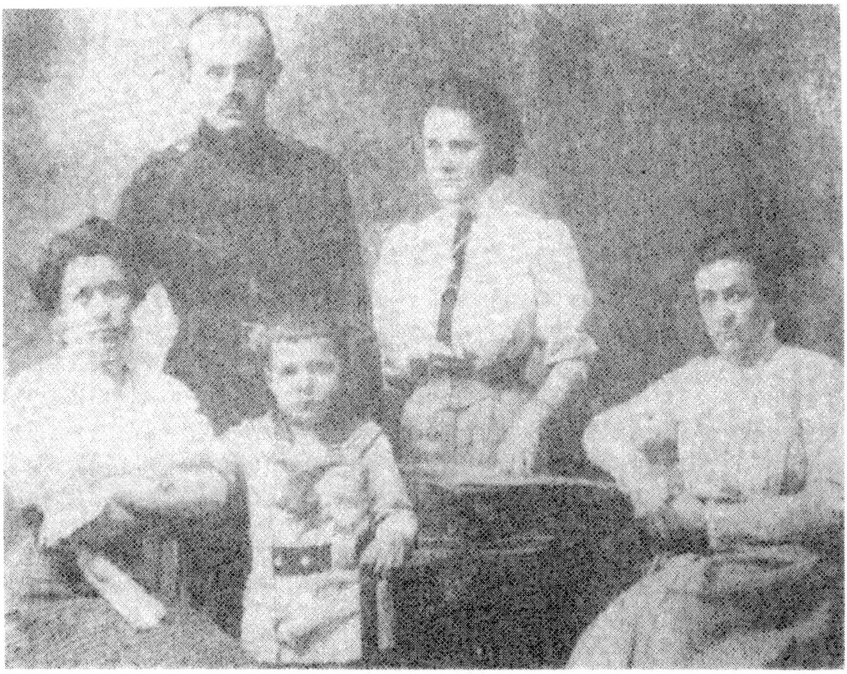

Picture 12: Mileva Einstein with her son and brother Miloš and sister Zorka

Albert was not against this baptism; he was, as Trbuhović said, relaxed and jovial. "Yesterday, my wife came from the holiday in Serbia with both of my children and with—do you know what effect? They have become orthodox Christians, and I am totally indifferent to that fact."

The Einsteins got along well with the Curies. This friendship was especially strong between Mileva and Marie Curie. The two women, the physicists, had something in common: They were both married to ingenious men, and they were both silent and sentimental, expressing an immense love for their husbands. Although Pier Curie died, Marie Curie kept loving her husband and magnifying his scientific work as if he was alive.

Marie Curie opened the door to ingenious inventions from radio-physics and chemistry, and Mileva Einstein searched into the secrets of quant theory. Frequently, they went for a walk together, and in 1913 they spent a couple of days on an excursion in the mountains. While these women talked cordially, Albert was having fun with the young governess of Marie Curie's daughter.

With time, Albert and Mileva had more and more disagreements. Mileva tried to remove all the impediments she encountered daily in her marriage, but it seemed to her that they were a long way from that harmonious relationship they had in Bern. She fought without compromise. Persistently and fervently she emphasized her love, fighting with dark forces that endangered her marriage ever more. When Albert got the transfer to Berlin, Mileva expressed her open dissatisfaction, demanding from him to reject the office and not to go to the foreign world. Einstein celebrated his thirty-fifth birthday on March 14, 1914 (he was born on March 14, 1879). He celebrated it with his wife and sons in Zurich. Mileva left to Locarno, afterward, for recuperation. The younger son, Eduard, had to go for recuperation after a serious illness. It was the reason why Einstein wanted to move to Berlin by himself. Mileva arrived a month later with the children. She was displeased and, for the first time in her life, she tried to make an open demand. At first, she inspired pity in Albert, but soon his feelings shifted and turned into hostility and disdain. He felt satisfied, full of irony and some strange courage, not feeling guilty at all that he lived on his own. Soon he made a decision to put everything in his marriage in order, and one day he took out of his pocket a book of rules and handed it to Mileva.

"You are obliged to stick to the following principles and rules," he wrote to his wife.

The book of rules:

A: 1. My clothing and my underclothing must always be clean. It is necessary that the food be brought to my study three times a day. My cabinet must always be in order, and apart from that, strange persons are not allowed to touch things on my desk. B: 1 You are obliged to give up the pretense of different relations with me, except those that are concerned with our image in the society, i.e., you will not demand from me: a) to spend my free time at home with you; b) to walk with you or to travel somewhere with you; C: you have to promise me exactly the following: 1. That you will not expect me to express my feelings and that you will not demand it, 2. That you will immediately and without postponement react to my addressing to you, 3. If I ask you to leave my cabinet, you will do that immediately and without remark, 4. That you will not underestimate me with words or acts before our children.

Mileva held the book of rules in her hands for hours. Albert had never seemed so strange and far to her as then. She did not understand what she had to do according to the book of rules, since she already did everything according to his will. While Mileva suffered, Albert exalted, taking huge steps to the success. She became a servant, without a remark.

AT THE END OF THE ROAD -THE LIGHT

I shall not examine the truth in this life,
and when I am united with you at last,
in the unity of the eternal primeval soul
of the world, I shall tell you as I always
did, "Great love of mine, you represented
all my life in a perfect way."

Berlin, the beginning of July 1914. Mileva did not know how to drive away her grief and how to forget about Albert's book of rules. She tried to forget about the offence, but she did not know what to change and what to do to please her beloved Albert. Everything that he mentioned in his book of rules, she had already been doing since long time, and she pleased him the best way she knew and could.

Mileva tried to think of some other things in order to forget and calm the painful feeling of solitude and suffering. She thought about her children, how grown up and how strong they were, and she also thought about her parents' home, about her past love, and the sweet words of Albert. She knew she must not bow her head, because then she would lose her dreams that were born each morning on a young horizon.

"I should not fear this situation. I should not suffer from this sick jealousy and because of the rules. He could not have meant what he wrote in that cruel book of rules," she consoled herself, realizing she should accept everything, be patient, endure, and drive away all the stupid thoughts that had been on her mind lately. However, there were moments when she wished to pack her things and go to Zurich with her children. On such occasions, she calmed and consoled herself that she should endure and stay in Berlin with her beloved husband. That was how Mileva sorted out her thoughts, not knowing what to do.

Those days in July, Berlin was a military town, and a general mobilization was declared. Germany and its ally Austria-Hungary were already largely preparing for the war. They wanted to fulfill their long-time wish to expand to Balkan Peninsula. In order to fulfill their ambition, they had to win Serbia first, by military force, because Serbia was on their way. The Kingdom of Serbia was at that time led by democratic hand of King Peter I, The Liberator, who was supported by the French, economically and politically.

After the amnesty of Bosnia and Herzegovina, Austria-Hungary wanted to fulfill its ambitious plan for conquering. War was being prepared largely in Berlin. Mobilized military force marched through the town and Mileva felt rather uncomfortable in it. She was worried about her brother and her people in Serbia, so she called some of her friends who lived in Austria Hungary.

On Sunday, some friends came for lunch and Mileva expected to hear some comforting words. However, she heard none. Her grievous feelings augmented even more. They said that the attempt of assassination in Sarajevo provoked disdain of lots of people who now unjustly and, whenever and wherever they could, blamed the Serbs in Serbia. A young friend of her brother, who was a student in Vienna, said that the Saturday before he had spoken to Count Traub Mansdorf, the chancellor of the embassy of Austria-Hungary. This man spoke of the terror of the "Serbian murders" and pointed out that it was the obligation of Austria-Hungary, in the interest of human kind and civilization, to stop, once and for all, the Serbian crime.

"His arrogant intonation," the young student said, "soon became unbearable. Two days after this conversation, the ambassador, Count Albert Mandorf, called me urgently for lunch, and this surprised me a lot.

"It is impossible for us to support Serbian provocations anymore. Serbia has to be punished. I hope the whole world will give us support in that matter."

Then, the young man immediately responded to the ambassador, "Austria-Hungary will then commit a suicide."

The ambassador smiled cynically and added, "Do you really believe that we, people of fifty million souls, are so weak that we cannot fight against a small nation such as Serbs, a nation that does not count more than three or four million people?"

"You certainly can trudge over Serbia," he told the ambassador, "but if the others let you do it. Even you will commit suicide. You have to count with a war of at least eight to nine months, with a mobilization of at least six hundred thousand people, approximately two hundred thousand dead and injured people and expenses of at least three billion crowns, which will ruin your finances. Do you know that Austria has been in debt for the last ten years, as your minister of finances said, a million crowns a day? Taxes are already so high that their further rising is impossible...When you conquer Serbia you will affront the problem of expensive military occupation that will require two hundred thousand people. If you annex Serbia, you will have a block of twelve million South Slavs whose aspirations will perturb the system of dualism to a great degree. In order to preserve its influence over you, Germany will demand and obtain such pledges of military, political and economical control that your independence will disappear."

"Are not Serbs in Hungary going to help us?" the ambassador asked in wonder.

The young man responded shortly, "By no means." (Mes souvenirs from H. V. Steed)

After this conversation, Mileva felt even more grievous and lonelier. She lived in a world of foreigners, far from her homeland, and all her friends remained in Zurich. In Berlin, that military town, she had only her children and her immense love for Einstein, who lived at that time in a world of his own. He acted as if Mileva and the children did not exist. He went out with unknown people, had new friends, and came home late at night. Admittedly, he was not interested in politics, and although he himself disliked this town full of marching soldiers, he did not want to leave Berlin.

Mileva dreamed of going back to Switzerland. She recalled wonderful days full of love and scientific work that she did with Albert. Mileva and Albert would not separate for months, but those days were long gone. Mileva still loved Albert—he was her life and her love—and she had a good reason to ask herself where the countless hours of scientific work had gone. She used to work day and night, cooking for the students in order to increase family budget. "Where had gone all those sweet words of my Albert, 'my sweetheart'? 'Erat should really have somebody like I do by his side' (Albert was proud of his wife).

"...When you become my dear wife, we shall work together, hard, in order not to convert into a couple of old people prone to philistine thinking, shall we not?" (The original letter from Albert Einstein from 1898).

All of these were just memories of past times. In Berlin, Mileva had no escape. Her beloved Albert was becoming more and more popular. He conquered the world with his charm and nice words, and she felt ever sadder and more and more miserable.

What strange forces ruled her world when everything was darkness, dominated by the missions from hell?

Paulina, Albert's mother, never accepted Mileva as her son's wife. She felt a strong, profound hatred towards Mileva.

The Einsteins, as a German family of Jewish origin, had tradition and pride, and they had always wanted Albert to marry a different kind of woman. Mileva tried hard to please them, to gain their approval. For a long time, Albert was caught in the middle, between his beloved Mitza and his mother, Paulina. Today, in Berlin, he fulfilled his mother's long-time wish. He loved no more the woman from the country of "Serbian rebels and bandits," as his respected mother, Paulina, used to say.

Even before, Albert saw some women in secret, here and there, but those were all transient relationships until he became intimate with his near relative Elsa. That was his mother's choice. Elsa soon became his secretary, although she was several years older than him as well (some people said she was two years, some five years older). Now it was not a matter of importance to his mother. Elsa's profession was acting; she liked applauding, fame, and money. A "shallow, superficial imitator" she was. Einstein, at that time, took huge steps towards success and, naturally, was obsessed with himself, with success, as well with philosophy and theoretical physics and all the joy this wonderful world offered.

Elsa, as an actress, knew well how to transform herself, to imitate, especially her Albert, seducing him with the identical voice, mimics, and sentences Albert produced. Albert was excited about the "acting" of hers, although it was a simple imitation. He could laugh with her, feel childish, neglecting the fact that Elsa was a woman of modest education, without spirit and without a firm line. A long time before, Albert had said about himself that he was fascinated by voices, his own as well with other people's voices. "I am the acoustic type: I learn with my sense of hearing, and I give the advantage to the words. Even when I read, I hear words. Writing is hard for me and I communicate with difficulty that way."

Mileva knew about this love affair between Albert and his cousin Elsa. It brought her despair, and she reproached herself for not having come to Berlin with her beloved Albert on March 29, 1914 (she had not come until the middle of April). It was already on July, when she felt week, without strength to fight; she felt lonely and depressive and saw Albert rarely. In some moments, it seemed that she would not stand the situation anymore.

For several days, she fought with herself; she had to reconcile sense and feelings. At last, she made a decision.

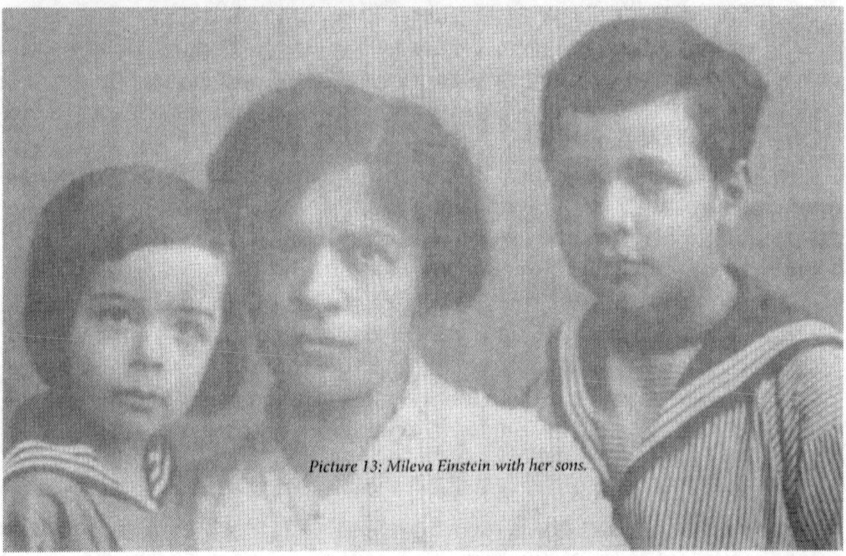

Picture 13: Mileva Einstein with her sons.

She would go back to Switzerland. The biographer of Albert Einstein, Armin Herman, said, "A faithful friend Michele Besso came from Switzerland to accompany Mileva and the children to Zurich. It was a sad procession towards the station."

Einstein cried only twice in his entire life: when his father died in 1912, and now when his family left. However, he certainly collected his thoughts soon, and then he felt indescribable pleasantness for finding himself again in the "palace of his mental peace." "I live completely alone in my big apartment and I can think uninterrupted," he wrote to Ehrenfest in Leiden. Some months afterward, he wrote, "The decision to isolate myself brought blessing to me." Einstein respected profoundly Ehrenfest's wife, Tatiana, hence he added, "You will not be able to understand this by any means."

Mileva carried with herself her painful memories from Berlin to Zurich. Her friend Lisbeth Hurwitz wrote in her diary about Mileva from that period, "At 4.30pm Mrs. Einstein came to us with her children for a cup of coffee. She is so pitiful. Since they are in Zurich, Einstein has become more and more alienated from his family, especially under the influence of a relative of his. I really do not know what is going to become of all of this. Children are so dear; the little one is especially lively and cheerful."

The Einstein family lived without the furniture that was left in Berlin.

Mileva had not paid the boarding house for quite a while, but she had not spoken to anybody about her difficult situation, and her husband was the only one whom she wrote about that.

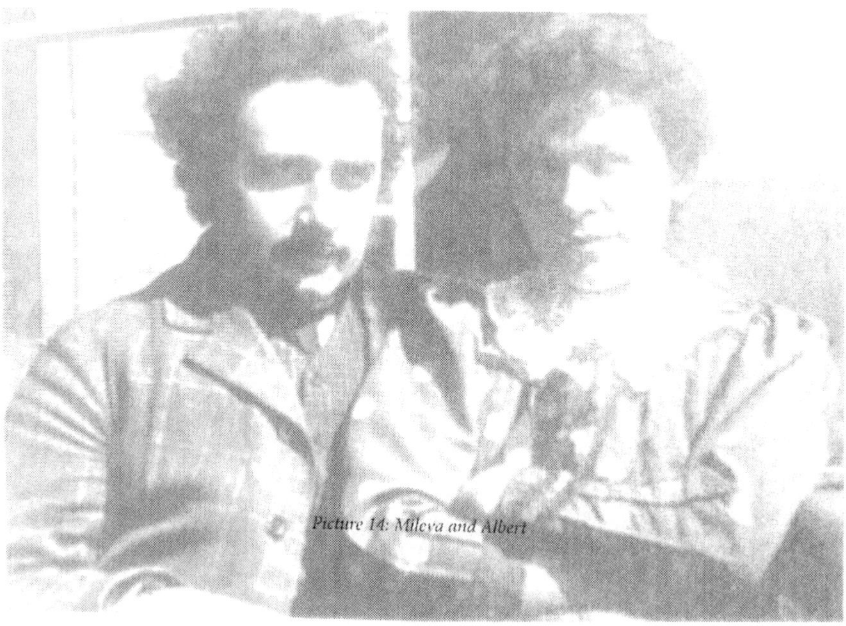

Picture 14: Mileva and Albert

"Proud as she was, she begged him, for the children, to send her the money regularly, because the children should not feel the misery at all. Mileva stole away with the boys when nobody was in the corridors." (Desanka Durić-Trbuhović)

She tried to collect her thoughts in all this misery of hers, not to withdraw without a fight, remembering how her father had said that she should not withdraw from the battles. Thus, she decided to try once again to recuperate the love of her beloved Albert.

Far away, in Berlin, Albert enjoyed in his solitude and he realized that the freedom was of utmost importance for him. After a couple of months, he decided to divorce Mileva, forever. When he came home one day, a year after Mileva's departure, she welcomed him cordially and cheerfully, and tried to convince her husband to continue to live with her.

"Come on," she said, "let us just forget about all the bad things. Come to Zurich to live with me and the children and give me one more opportunity to show you how much I love you." All the guilt and misunderstandings in their marriage she put on herself, not knowing what was that she should change in herself. However, Mileva knew that he moved to Elsa's and she knew that Albert now was Elsa's.

Albert was taken by surprise as he heard these words, and curtly he said, "A bunch of nonsense. My world, I am positive, is going to be better off without you."

Mileva froze at these words; her face became pale, her eyes brimming with tears. Barely audibly, she whispered, "I anticipated that it would terminate like this. I shall move out as early as tomorrow, if you wish."

Albert jumped up from the sofa on which he had just sat. For a moment it seemed he vacillated, but eventually he spoke cruelly: "That is much better."

However, Mileva still did not quit, staying, "You, my dear, you will forever have a place in my life."

Albert did not respond to these cordial words but instead pulled out, in one abrupt move, a huge piece of paper and handed it to her. "This is the list of the things that belong to you and the children and that you can carry away with you as far as tomorrow."

Mileva took the long list:

1. Your mirror from Titel
2. Dining room
3. Wardrobe closet
4. Green armchair
5. A* b*š

She just could not read any more; everything blurred in front of her eyes and the tears did not let her see anything. The letters blurred and mixed. She sat at the corner of the room, on the green armchair, and stayed there until the morning, with the list in her hand.

Since the early morning, the servants had packed the things, according to Einstein's list, and the porter took them to the carriage. Afterwards, he transported them to the other house, far away from the life that the married couple Einstein used to have together. Mileva sat all the time, without saying a word, profoundly in her thoughts, almost unaware of the people around her. Her eyes were sad, as if they had absorbed all the grief of this world.

The porter of the furniture felt pity for her. "Poor woman, she looks so sad, as if she had already stepped into some other world." They raised her from the green armchair, since it was on the list as well.

The carriage with the Einstein family slid silently across the paved streets of Zurich. One could hear nothing but the thud of the hooves echoing in an empty street. The sad carriage was ever farther from the old home.

That is how Mileva said goodbye to her life spent together with her beloved Albert.

The children chatted with the servant along the way, describing their new house. "In a second we shall see our new house, right here, around the corner!" the elder son Hans shouted. After a few moments, they really saw their new home, in a narrow street.

The house was situated at the corner of the street. It had a white facade and was garnished in a baroque style. It was high, as well, with the mansard and a little, square yard. Silent, Mileva stood at the door of her new home with the children and the servant (who was hired by Albert just for a while).

The children liked the house and, cheerful, they started to call it "our new home." Mileva still sat for days in that green armchair and the grief augmented. All the pain in her womb she transformed into a rock.

The First World War had already begun, and her brother was at the battlefield, mobilized as an Austro-Hungarian soldier. He was sent to Russian front, and she had not heard from him for a long, long time.

The Marić family felt all the grief of the world. Austro-Hungarian military authorities put on a board a list of names of the deserters, among whom was Miloš Marić, Mileva's brother, whom she loved immensely. It was a moment when she lost her brother as well.

For days she sat in solitude in a small room in the mansard. Her heart was torn by grief and solitude.

The children were taken care of by her friend Helena and other friends who took children to their home, from time to time, in order to help Mileva until she was recuperated. Each day she anticipated the summons for the divorce. She lived, thus, in fear concealed from the eyes of the world. She nursed her grief as the greatest blessing of her heart, in a spectral, white, and infinite void. The void filled her whole being, surrounding her completely as the chains of death.

She sat at the corner of the room, in the green armchair, gazing at the white circle on the carpet, which was her only connection with the world. Her thought slipped through the void without a way out, and her love towards Albert turned into a large, bloody wound of her heart. It was late fall already, and she still was not recuperated. Friends said about her, "She is profoundly depressed; who knows how she is going to come over all of this."

The health condition of Mileva Einstein was critical. She could barely walk. Emotions and unfulfilled wishes aggravated her health. She whispered barely audibly, "How shall I live without you, Albert, how?" Tears flew down her pale face in a stream. She sat in her room, long forgotten by her beloved Albert.

It was a cold day in fall, one of those sad days when golden leaves wear their dark brown coats and the nightingales' song was deafened by cawing crows mourning the dying nature.

Just for a moment, a strong wind lifted a bunch of umber, muddy leaves, dragging it over a long street and making piles in front of the green house opposite to Mileva's window.

The street had a stone sidewalk on one side only, and it was so narrow that two pedestrians could hardly pass at the same time. There was nobody in the street who slumbered in a fall haze, empty and sprinkled with raindrops.

Fall rain made Mileva's heart grieve even more. Their big love was now dwelling in a flower girdle of dead past, which became the monument of suffering in pale emptiness, luring her into death's icy, cold embrace.

She chased away from her heart every beautiful image of love for her children, life, and friends. She had no reason to live. "I am lost without Albert," she whispered. She was like candle in the wind, flickering back and forward defenselessly, in a sad echo of eternity.

Pale ghosts, masters of midnight obscurity, gave her a glass of illusion to drink to the bottom and so bereaved her of her very being. She heard, from the emptiness deep inside her soul, the sounds of past shadows echoing bluntly as if from the vast hell, "He had left me for another woman; he had left me for another woman."

Large tears burnt her eyes and face. Physical pain reminded her that she was still alive. She heaved her tired, painful body and, limping and waddling, approached the window. Easily, with a painful hand, she lifted the short white curtain.

The rain outside was still soaking the facades of the houses that, being wet, looked old and ghastly. Her eyes dwelled upon the green house across the street, and it brought the past back to her for a moment. The big gate of the house reminded her of the one in Novi Sad, of her childhood, and of long-forgotten time.

She watched the gate with melancholic eyes for a long time that day, as if she wanted to say goodbye to her native soil. On the both sides of the gate, there were figures of lions, whose eyes glittered so strangely that it seemed to Mileva she was looking at the death itself. Suddenly, the thought of death filled her with happiness. Walking silently and shakily, she approached the cupboard and took out a hidden poison bottle that she had bought in Berlin, at the time when Albert had given her those "rules." She had been overwhelmed with thoughts of death at that time, but they had not bothered her again until today.

Today, she was empty, with no thoughts and wishes. Time, her children, and her life did not exist for her any longer. It was her eternal, immeasurable, obscure love that existed only. She only wanted to live with the man of her life.

"I will die for you, my love," she whispered, gazing at the rainy street.

Teardrops sparkled in her eyes. Raindrops, vibrating and falling from tarnished leaves of the old chestnut tree, blended with the image of her beloved man. Death was only a few seconds away. Somehow, Mileva straightened herself as a statue. Leaning on the window, she stared at that big, vaulted entrance across the street, wishing to say goodbye for the last time to her father and mother. She wanted to justify herself, for she had lost that battle of love.

In a few moments, she would drink up the poison and leave this world silently, unobstructed and unnoticed, taking with her all her grief, sorrow, and painful memories.

Suddenly, she was roused from her mortal thoughts. By the gate Mileva was staring at, a beggar woman appeared with an empty bag over her shoulder and with a little child in her arms. She started to pace up and down and to peek through the gate, looking for the doorbell. Then, she turned around abruptly, as if to someone's order, and looked up straight at Mileva's wet, deadly eyes.

It seemed to Mileva that the beggar's eyes were so close that she could see her own reflection in them. By "destiny's will," she saw in those eyes the struggle for piece of bread, the struggle for that little child in the arms.

At that moment, she was overwhelmed with anxiety, not for the woman, but for the child, who reminded her for a second of their Lieserl.

The beggar woman found the doorbell rope and pulled it so vehemently that all surrounding houses started to shake from that peal.

A young, beautiful woman, whose bosoms were overflowing her tight dress, came out of the house. Her hair was curled into a bun; her round face was beautiful but strict. She chased away the beggar woman gruffly and abusively, and disappeared quickly.

Mileva felt sorry for the beggar woman. She opened the window and silently invited her to enter the house. The beggar woman stepped away, hesitated for a moment, and then, stunned by that unexpected generosity, ran through the ground floor narrow door separated by two arcades with two Roman crosses from the eighteenth century on them. With quick steps, she started to mount steep, wooden stairs, grabbing the staircase with her rough hands. Her quick steps made the whole house shake, as if a flock of children invaded the house. In a few seconds, she stood in front of Mileva. Mileva saw that the woman was shapely and beautiful. She wore a black and violet dress with big flowers and a shawl, although it was chilly fall weather outside.

Mileva took a warm sweater and a jacket out of her closet and together with bread, meat, and some money for little "Lieserl" gave all that to the woman. "Let me hold her for a moment," asked Mileva with the pain in her voice. The beggar woman gave her the child for a moment.

Mileva stretched her arms towards the past and poked ancient flames in her soul. Just for a second, she was again little Lieserl's beloved mother, whom Albert had written:

Dear Dokserl (Dolly),

I am not in the least angry at poor Dokserl (Dolly) hatching new chick. Actually, I am happy because of it and I thought it could be another Lieserl. Finally you should not be deprived of every woman's right; do not worry about that and come back to me satisfied. Take care of him tenderly so that everything ends up well...Come back as soon as possible.

Kisses, Jochanzel (Johnny)

Somewhere from sad subconsciousness, the lines of this letter came out, and she thought for a second, *Still, he might have loved me once.*

That was the first thought that connected Mileva with actual world. New hope enlightened her mind and made her alive again. Nevertheless, she noticed that vast desert remained in her heart, painfully reminding her of her unfulfilled love.

From that waste part of her heart, she could step into bridge of wishes and touch those happy, loving times with Albert; she could give herself up to imagination and live again in the past, in the dreams that existed only in her mind.

After those suicidal intentions, she did not resist her dreams any longer. They became secret dwellers of her mind and part of her life. It was pointless to fight them. She was ill. She walked with difficulties and spoke rarely, spending her hours in silence and absorbed in her own contemplation. The family was in distress, burdened with existential problems. Mileva was ill during the war and Albert did not care.

Many friends forgot her, many friends turned to the famous Albert Einstein. She was going towards another world, a world without wealth and fame. She wended her way, walking unevenly, with no hope for better future in her heart. An uncertain financial situation oppressed the Einsteins. It seemed that their sufferings would never end.

Many years later, Hans Albert told Đoiđe Krstić, a journalist, about that difficult period of distress and abandonment. Mr Krstić said, "Their son Hans Albert confided to me that those years had been the most difficult for them. Albert had been living with Elsa at that time, and although he was well off and with enormous salary, he had hardly sent any money to his children. Hans Albert had many bitter recollections of those hard days and lonely hours, when his mother had been forced to borrow money from others."

It was the moment when Mileva began to dig up the past buried in her mind. Thus she sat, ill as she was, for hours, months, and years. She was gravely ill for four years, gazing absently in a vast space that only she could see.

A friend wrote to Albert, advising him not to divorce Mileva because she was extremely depressed at that time. She could hardly get out of her bed because of her sick leg.

Albert decided, "I will postpone the divorce for two years, until she gets well a bit and forgets me."

A mutual friend told Mileva of Albert's decision, but she did not say a word, only a dark shadow of pain crossed her face. She thought, unawares, *Is it the same man whom I opened the door of miraculous and wonderful world of science? How could he forget big goals and accept the fame only?*

In August and September 1917, Mileva was in the hospital. She asked her mother to come to Zurich and take care of her, but her mother was ill, so she sent Mileva's sister Zorka.

Zorka came to Zurich at the beginning of October and started to study biology.

Hard life conditions in Vojvodina during the First World War, blood, sufferings, the disappearance of their brother, and many other troubles that befell the Marić family, had a bad influence on the beautiful girl Zorka. She started to express general suspicion towards the outside world and people, and as time was passing by, she started to hate them. Soon, she had visible signs of mental illness, and Mileva asked their father to come and take Zorka home, which he did.

At the end of 1917, Albert Einstein was offered to come back to Zurich. He refused it but held a series of lectures there in 1918. He lived in a hotel at that period but visited Mileva and his children regularly. Mileva was reserved to her husband, but somewhere deep inside her soul she secretly hoped that he would come back to her.

The First World War was still raging, but the end of it could be anticipated. It was the time when sorrow and fear mixed with happiness and joy. The end of the war brought pain to Mileva, because her brother never returned from Russia.

Now, she was able to look more objectively on her and Albert's mutual past. She knew that no wind of love could change the course of her life. *Nothing similar will ever happen to me,* Mileva thought. *A rocky desert is inside me now.* She meditated on her past life she could not reach anymore and on her unuttered pain; she resisted those blows of fate all by herself.

She did not want anybody's charity anymore. She was still suffering. She felt the eternal thirst of Tantalus. She was aware of her life, of the tragic fate that was inevitable. Now, she accepted it without resistance.

Albert's lover, Elsa, wanted him to divorce Mileva as soon as possible. Anyway, he had long forgotten Mileva and she was dead for him.

Finally, on February 14, 1919, the divorce was completed, without the presence of the Einsteins. "Incompatibility of characters" was noted as the cause of the divorce. The Einsteins' divorce contract envisioned that the complete sum of the Nobel Prize, awarded to Albert and Mileva Einstein for their research, was to be given to Mileva.

Albert's biographer, Armin Herman, wrote: "After he divorced Mileva, Albert did not occupy her thoughts and feelings any more. While she was suffering because of the divorce, Einstein felt better than ever. 'I slumber peacefully with calm thoughts and what I feel is a kind of mixed remorse and repulsiveness,' he said."

Einstein was self-satisfied, paving the paths of glory. He gave lectures, was engaged in politics, and became more and more successful every day. Soon, he became the most popular scientist of the time. It was the time when he mounted the world's scientific peak, but without Mileva Einstein. He felt an extreme need for music and for all the pleasures life could offer. In order to show his humanism, he played at many charity concerts. He could play Mozart brilliantly, so his admirers used to say, "A great man is great at everything he does."

His dear boys, as he called them, were now young men and did not get along well with their father. Especially Hans Albert was dissatisfied with his father's negligent behavior. He was already fifteen and bluntly showed hostile attitude towards his father.

Soon after he divorced Mileva, in summer 1919, urged by his mother and aunt, he married his close cousin, Elsa.

Elsa already had two daughters, whom Albert later adopted as his own children. He lived far away from his true family, giving them very poor allowances.

Life was full of pain for Mileva even before the divorce, but since she divorced, she felt life as a heavy burden threatening to fall on her head and suffocate her.

She remembered how her father had taught her battle tactics.

"In special circumstances, you must force your enemy to retreat; changing the way of fighting can sometimes bring the success."

Mileva smiled at those distant words her father had used as morals for successful life. She wondered what she did of her life. She knew that she had all lawful rights on her scientific works with Albert. She had those rights as his associate as well as his wife. Her name should have stood beside Albert's; it would have been righteous and completely understandable, it would have been natural law of cosmic existence. Such thoughts provoked in her a sudden fit of helplessness, and her whole body started to shake and she started to cry and sob, uttering silently the words, "No, I cannot do that to him. We existed on a higher level of scientific life. I bestowed on him my whole past, present, and future."

It was February, a few days after the divorce. Mileva was sitting alone in the house. With nobody there, she could freely indulge herself in her feelings and painful memories, trying once again to collect herself, to reconsider, and to decide. What kind of fight could she enter with Albert? She painfully realized that fighting with Albert would be fighting with herself. Suddenly, she was full of spite, even hatred, and she wanted to win everybody over, to crush and annihilate them, and so prove her greatness and her scientific perfection. For a moment, she forgot her kindness, charity, and love. She decided to fight them all.

Suddenly, she realized that she came to an end of her scientific journey. She left only secret traces on the world's horizon. Now, she wanted to forget everything and to leave everything on the smooth surface of the "world's soul."

She sat in front of the mantelpiece, lonely and abandoned, pressing her hands with her knees, and looking absently at the fire that crackled while fingers of flame licked the logs. She looked at it absently for a long time, and past memories flooded back to her. She felt extreme pain, memories tortured her, and she felt something like a premonition; it would be the moment of her great decision.

She knew that, had her love been of this world, she would have still been Einstein's wife. She recollected how he had taken from her the discipline at work, seriousness, and the way of recovering work energy. Mileva used to work highly concentrated on new complex mathematical constructions, even for twelve hours. Albert was proud of her and he would tell his colleagues, "My Mitza is a Perpetuum Mobile of the second kind."

That flow of memories made her take out a big orange box where she kept all original documents about their joint work when they were one family: the Einsteins. There were those numerous drafts and outlines, original manuscripts of the relativity theory, and her correspondence with Albert. There were his photographs...there was all her life there. Something stirred up inside her, and she wished to tell someone the truth about her life. She wished to reveal everything and to put her name beside the name of her beloved Albert. However, at that very moment, the words of Socrates' speech from his trial in 399 B.C. appeared in front of her eyes,

"My honorable man...You are the greatest man of wisdom, glory and power, but you are not ashamed to pile the treasure for glory and honor. Yet, you do not care much to enhance your mind and soul."

Somehow, there emerged an old story told by the teacher and the priest from Karlovci of how one should bathe in the river of oblivion and so wash away all the troubles of this world.

Then, she felt the need to forget everything and to say goodbye to her past. She started to revise the papers with her mathematical proves. First, she examined the paper no. 1, then paper no. 2, no. 3...then she started reading them.

Mileva took the paper where there was only one sentence, written by the hand of her beloved Albert.

> I mastered the following method:
>
> I exclude difficult problems and solve the easy ones.
>
> Mitzy, your Jochanzel (Johnny) loves you

Mileva lifted the second paper with grief but with dignity and started reading it as if she was reading the most sacred biblical words.

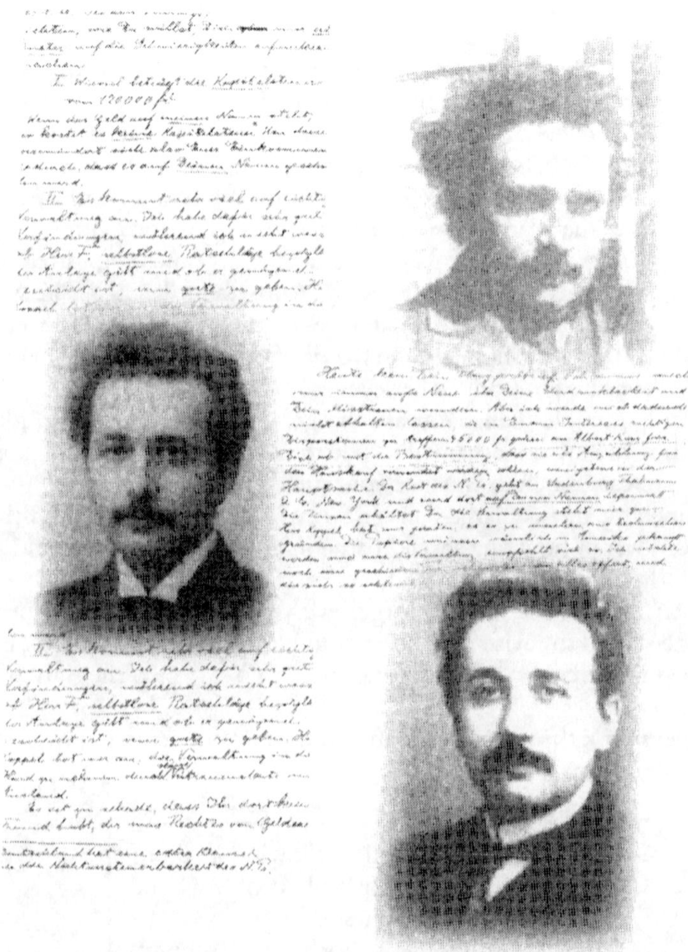

At once, she decided she would burn everything down. With a shaky hand, she was throwing papers into fire, one by one, and then threw into fire a bunch of different papers, notes, and calculations and felt satisfied to see that everything turned into ashes in front of her eyes.

She gave to the universe all her scientific speculations.

"What about us?" Mileva asked herself quietly.

Out of the orange box, she took letters and photographs of her beloved Albert Einstein and decided that it all should become past. Let it all turn to dust! She grabbed the letters and threw them into fire that blazed. Flames flicked and roared. When Mileva saw her beloved's face burning and turning into a pile of ash, she screamed, hailed God, and with bare hands poked into the fire to save the pictures of her beloved man. However, all efforts were in vain; soon she noticed that her hands were burnt and her heart was terribly aching.

She felt strong dizziness as if she was losing consciousness. The room started to whirl around her and soon became a dark tunnel where she fell in as if pushed by somebody.

She was overwhelmed with a great fear because of the speed she was passing through the tunnel, while her body was falling on sharp Roman spears. When it seemed to her that the spears would pierce her body and that the death was knocking on the door, the spears spaced and Mileva slowly fell on a luminescent plateau. She was safe there and somehow happy in a strange way. Her eyes roamed the infinite space of heaven and saw a milky white gleam and herself floating in it. Down there, on the Earth far away, beside the mantelpiece, lay her physical body with burnt hands.

Just for a moment, she was not sure if she was alive or her soul moved to another world. She was happy and perfectly calm, realizing that she was just a tiny fragment of the eternal soul and that her thoughts were mingled with stars in the eternal light. She saw vast galaxies, perceiving that she, as a unit, was involved in a timeless process of development towards higher levels of consciousness. While she was floating on the celestial level of knowledge, it occurred to Mileva that she could see her past lives.

Suddenly, she saw her beginning far behind, deep, strong, and impressive, the first life of her soul in the sinful body of a Roman emperor who had been honored, powerful, glorious, and famous at that time. She identified with the beginning of her existence. In her mind, she saw the picture of herself as a leader of the Roman army, upright and proud emperor in togs flapping in the wind while the people had cheered happily, "Viva, viva, viva..."

After many centuries, she turned back in the sinful body and felt all the bitterness of glory and sin in which her soul had been captivated when she had opened Pandora's Box with the Roman spear. From that life, her soul brought sin and forbidden glory, and only then, on the celestial level, did she realize where all those restrictions, grief, bitterness, and sufferings had come from. Her soul traveled through numerous lives of worldly time, conveying to each of it the same idea of purification and complete happiness and eternal endless love.

Just for a moment, she thought that she reached her destination, that she achieved her goal through eternal, immeasurable love for Albert Einstein. She saw flowery meadows, the beauty of infinity, and she felt the happiness in zephyr. She heard secret, enchanting music; she heard her beloved Albert playing. Suddenly, the music turned into a call; something lured her into a heavenly valley of love. Blissful scents of blossoming herbs intoxicated her soul, and warm feelings of love filled her entire mind. Mileva was already far away from her mortal body, floating as a shadow through the space of heaven, over the boundaries of the worlds, and on the line between life and death. She stood in front of the St. John's gate, and suddenly, as if she was waiting for the verdict, she did not know if she should pass the heavenly gate and enter the translucent, heavenly valley of love. She looked back once again, into the dark tunnel she had come from, and then happened what was meant to happen as a proof that the fate existed: In the obscurity of despair, she saw her lifeless body and her sons sorrowfully mourning over it. She heard her house cleaner crying the prayers to the Heavens, to the God, and the God's mother that Mileva's soul must not die. She cried that Mileva must not leave her children alone and unprotected. Hans Albert and Tete-Eduard cried sadly, kissing their beloved mother's face. When Mileva's soul saw that unhappy scene, it forgot the heavenly valley of love it intended to enter from the eternal heaven's plateau. Then, she felt an irresistible desire to turn back, realizing that her children needed her presence the most. She realized how wrong her conclusions had been. Love for children is the last link to the pure light, and the entrance of the world's ancient soul. Mileva learnt that from somewhere. She accepted her destiny and her soul reentered her physical body immediately.

When she opened her eyes, she saw her sons. She gently whispered, "My sons, you are my life, you are my whole world." They cried happy tears, kissed her, and jumped playfully around her. Mileva saw her burnt hands and felt strong pain, but she did not care for it.

A small pile of letters she did not manage to burn was lying beside her. She reached them and, with painful hands, hid them for future generations. *Let the letters show how great my beloved Albert's love was,* she thought. After she died, these letters were found among Mileva's possessions. Thanks to Mileva's granddaughter, Elena, the daughter of Hans Albert, these letters have been saved until today.

Mileva's burnt hands healed with time, but the effects of the heart attack and the unconsciousness remained. She was in bed for four days, and when doctors thought her life came to an end, her wounds healed and she recuperated.

From that day on, nothing was the same.

What once had been the most important thing for Mileva, the struggle for love, now was excluded as an unwelcome thought. She had other matters to deal with, her children at the first place. Mileva raised the children. Albert let her do it, saying that he confided in her. She was very generous and good-humoured as a mother. She was full of understanding for her sons; she smiled with them and participated in their school worries. She never spoke to anyone about her pain and distress. When she recovered from her illness, she tutored mathematics and music (she gave piano lessons). Little spare time she had, she dedicated to plant breeding. She was especially fond of cactuses.

She was not in contact with Albert. Neither did he interfere with the children's upbringing, nor did he take any care of them. When he finally got the Nobel Prize, "awarded to Albert Einstein," he gave the complete sum to Mileva and so proved their everlasting, eternal unity. The children rejoiced in the success of the Einstein family. Mileva bought two houses in Zurich for her sons with a part of the Nobel Prize award money.

Hans Albert was a playful, mischievous boy. He even fought with other boys while spending his summer holidays in Novi Sad. Younger Tete was gentle and amiable, and everybody loved him. According to some claims, Albert was rather rude with his children and they did not bring him any happiness, or at least he told his friends something like that.

Hans Albert became an engineer. He graduated from the Technical College in Charlottenburg. According to some facts, a firm that made projects for Bridge of King Tomislav, built in 1928 over the Danube in Novi Sad from the funds of the German war reparations from the First World War, used Hans Albert's graduation work as a layout. Albert Einstein thought it was not good that Hans Albert became an engineer. "I wanted at first to become a man of techniques," he explained to his friend Heinrich Zanger. "It was an unsupportable idea that I should spend my ability to make innovations, the things that would make everyday life more subtle, and that I should struggle for money." He complained to his friend that his son inherited from him the laziness for writing, which he had inherited from his father, "That is, actually, the only 'inheritance' that you get in my family, along with some intellectual capabilities and a certain degree of spite."

Hans Albert came of age on May 14, 1925. Soon after that, he decided to marry Eva, ten years his senior. Albert disapproved of that marriage. He said that it was not love but suggested compulsion. He called his future daughter-in-law an ugly old woman and a rather small goitrous creature, and above all, her mother was in a mental institution.

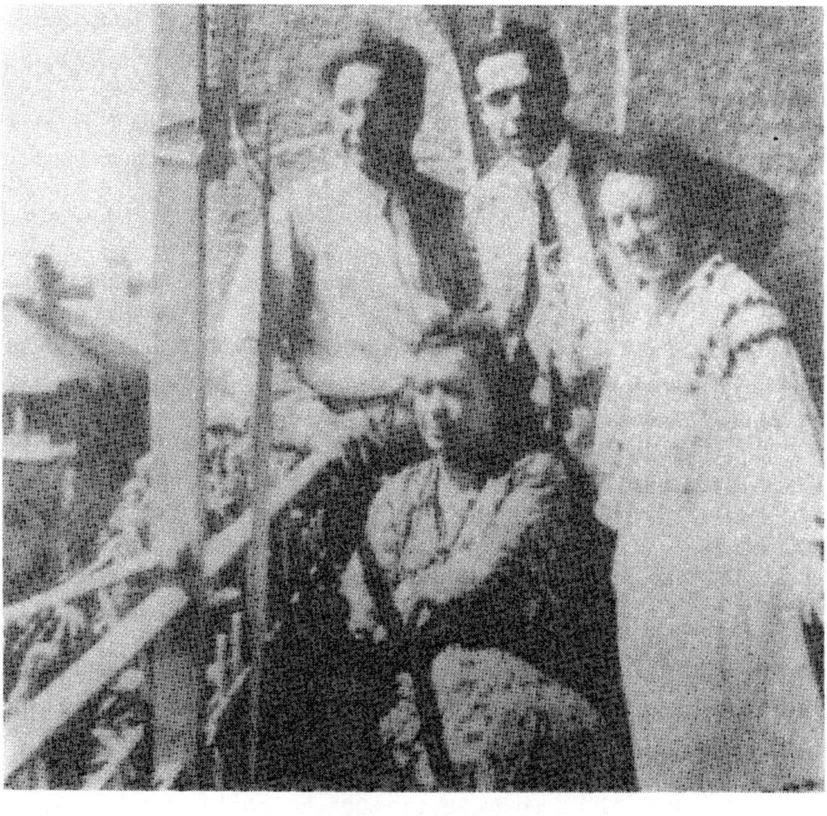

Picture 15: Mileva with her sons and her daughter-in-law

Younger son Tete-Eduard, who was very sensitive with delicate health, loved books very much. He wrote poems and played Bach by heart. He graduated from the high school in 1929 and entered a medical college, but he had to terminate his studies at the very beginning because of his illness.

Since that sad moment, when Mileva had burnt everything and changed her life, she was unusually joyous; she was happy for having her sons. She never again mentioned her wonderful, sensual love for Albert Einstein. She spoke of him exclusively as of a father of her sons. She never again mentioned scientific works. Only once, she told her sister that she handed over to God all her acquired knowledge. She mixed it with the Universe and they became one.

Plato had said, "Pleasure cannot be given to God, but the knowledge can." According to him, a pure soul should have reasoning wisdom, brave spirit, and perfected moderation. Mileva had all three.

She knew that her soul had already traversed the larger part of its journey, and that the future should last shortly until it reached "pure perfection" and entered the Almighty being.

Her whole past and numerous disapprovals and argues with her beloved Albert disappeared for her forever. Now, she knew better than ever that her eternal love was fruitful ground for the relativity theory. Now that everything was over, she used to say, "One dream disappeared in touch with reality."

Love was that outer power that worked for Mileva and Albert, and their inner being bore a new offset of the providential idea that merged in eternal unity called EINSTEIN.

Although they agreed to divorce, Mileva and the children kept the surname Einstein, at Albert's suggestion. In that way, Mileva remained united with the immortal part, with the name of Einstein.

However, it was all past. She accepted life as it was, and she knew that one woman could reach the happiness through genuine love for husband, children, and science.

She did not want to judge her past severely. The only experience she had was her memory that she would carry with her in the future.

The desperation of the past days was far behind her. Now, she confided deeply in the Universe. The illusory hope that her beloved man would return did not exist any longer. She knew that she broke through the wall of "life secrets" and that a boundary "wall" connected her with the eternity. She erased it with great, unselfish love and it was, for Mileva, the most valuable thing worth living for, apart from the scientific glory.

Now, the days were flying shadows passing by her. She devoted all her being, thoughts, love, expectations, and fears to her sons, rejoicing their visits. Her sons had their own lives, and Mileva was lonely. She dedicated herself to a new path of knowledge; she uncovered the path of darkness and found new aim in her earthly torturing. She loved to read, especially physics. She wanted to keep pace with all researches, but mostly she read philosophical books, where she tried to find some answers from everyday life.

Hans Albert finished his studies, got a job, and rarely visited his mother in Zurich. Tete started to study medicine (when he fell ill, his bodyguard took him to lectures).

Her son rarely came home together, at the same time, but when it happened Mileva was thrilled and happy. She used to make cakes and clean the house days in advance, rejoicing in those happy moments. When she was expecting her sons to visit her, time was passing very slowly and she did not know how to free her mind of that eager anticipation. She was trying to fight it all the time, but moments became hours, and hours were endless. She prepared herself for her sons' arrival, feeling immeasurable happiness and forgetting the emptiness of her life. The translucent light of happiness could be seen on her face; she forgot her illness, lame leg, and all other troubles. Her whole heart rejoiced the arrival of her children.

However, the happiness did not last long. She noticed, very soon, visible mental health problems of her younger son, which turned later into an incurable disease and a psychological disorder. One day, when Mileva suddenly entered her son's room, which was pasted over with pornographic pictures and usually silent, she heard some strange humming and mumbling. Her younger son Eduard produced those mysterious sounds. He was confused, lost. Signs of astonishment, doubt, and mental disturbance were visible on his face. She approached her son gently, but he acted as if he did not recognise her. He mumbled some noiseless, dull, and unrecognisable words.

The poor mother tried to comfort him, and it occurred to her, "How I miss my Albert now. He would know what to do or to say to help our dear, sick child, whose psyche is obviously overburdened."

Even before this accident, Eduard was gentle, sensitive, shy, and of poor physical health. He was now expressing visible signs of mental disturbance, although he was peacefully sitting and watching the world around him. Mileva consulted Hans Albert about what to do, and they decided to call the doctor. He gave some medicines to the young man and promised to call on in a couple of days and examine him again.

However, Eduard's disturbed mind, in the fear of its dark thoughts, regarded the suicide as the only solution. On a dark night, after a turbulent day, he locked himself in his room and started to bang violently and to throw things all over the room in desperation. His mother implored him to open the door, and when he finally did it, he was all ragged and distraught. He wanted to end his sufferings. The window on the third floor was wide open, and his small and weak mother used her utmost forces to prevent strong, insane young man to approach it. Eduard took it all out on her; he threw on her everything that was within his reach, and finally he grabbed her frail neck and pressed it with his hands. For a few moments, Mileva looked death in the face, but he managed to collect himself at the very last minute. The poor mother, staggering and pronouncing words with difficulties, called the ambulance, not for herself but for her sick boy.

Eduard was brought into a mental institution after that suicide attempt. There, in the darkness of his thoughts, he lived for the rest of his life.

When she put her son in the institution, she visited her husband in Berlin, which she had never done before. She found Albert happy with his new family. That day was the wedding day of his adoptee, Elsa's daughter.

In front of the City Hall, where the wedding was about to take place, many people were waiting to see the famous scientist, Einstein. Mileva was standing in the middle of that crowd, eyes wide open; great pain of the whole world was visible on her face.

Einstein passed by her calmly, as if he did not see her. Mileva did not call him, because she did not want to ruin somebody else's happiness with her misery. Later that day, she met Albert and asked him to unite their forces and help their sick son.

Eduard adored his father, and the lack of domestic environment was, for sure, one of the reasons of the mental disturbance of this sensitive boy; he showed strange, passionate love for his father. That adoration and wish to identify with his father in everything, and especially in success and fame, made him desperate.

When Eduard realized that his father had abandoned him for good, he tried to commit suicide and thus solve all his problems.

Talking to Albert, there in Berlin, Mileva implored her husband, for the last time in her life, to help her, but he calmly refused to give her a hand, concluding that it was all the matter of heredity. Mileva could not see the end of her troubles. Hans Albert worked in the USA, and so she was left alone with her dead past, sad present, and pointless future.

Again, the dark forces exiled the divine spark for the millionth time.

Alone and abandoned, Mileva suffered profoundly for her son.

Eduard was in a mental institution, gravely ill. She was not able to visit him for a while. She could not do nothing else but wait. She did not go out anymore. Mileva lived in a house behind a high fence of intertwined ivy leaves that stretched all over the wall. She alienated herself from the rest of the world, in the house surrounded by grassy yard. A nice avenue of trees stretched along a wide path of crushed stone, leading to the terrace. She used to spend her lonely hours there. It seemed as if she was waiting for somebody. Her face was anxious, serious, and withered, with deep wrinkles, the scars of life. Her thoughts were swarming, and finally they turned into a plane prayer of a mother silently addressing Madonna to help her sick child.

Days full of pain were passing slowly. People say that fate, like dreams, can be recognized by some signs. The misfortune that Eduard suffered from enchained Mileva's soul with iron grief and turned Mileva's body into material prison of her soul. She lived sad and lonely. She spent her days in grief and prayers for her son. She prayed that her son would recuperate, and that he would be able to recognize her and accept her motherly love. She visited her son every day, trying to calm and enlighten his schizophrenic mind. She was trying to teach him how to survive in those cramped hospital rooms, and how to rejoice when he saw her, his mother, who was the world for him. She understood the laws of the Universe, which creates, preserves, and finally destroys everything.

Tete would come back home from the hospital for several days, but his bodyguard was always with him. Tete liked to play instruments, but it was such a cacophony and he made such a noise that neighbours complained abut the loudness from the Einsteins' house. It was the moment when he would be taken him back to hospital.

Mileva lived alone in Zurich, far away from her homeland.

The morning had just broken. It was spreading and waving over the endless firmament above the sleepy town of Zurich. Thin rays of flickering light, transformed into myriads of particles, made a new day. In the middle of a big town, but yet far away from the rest of the world, there lived a lonely woman who accepted the first whispers of the morning, aware that she was getting old. For quite a while that morning, she looked at the big mirror on the wall, which her grandmother had given her long time ago for her fifteenth birthday. Unawares, she remembered her reflection in the mirror, happy and radiant at that time. *Now, only my eyes retained that gleam of youth,* she thought, watching the image of her aging face in the oak framed mirror, made by a crafty hand of a Viennese artisan. First, she gently caressed her face, and then, with her withered hand she embraced the mirror as if she was embracing her Kać, her Titel, and all her family. It was her secret link with past, but it already faded away in her memory. Now, she was far away from those marvellous days of youth. She felt that, every part of her body, in spite of her illness and need for rest, became slave of her grand maternal love. Then, she regained her determination, grit, and willingness to succeed and to surmount all the obstacles. She wanted to help her sick son with her own forces, discerning what could and what could not be changed. She wanted to protect him as much as she could, remembering how her father had protected her when some children had shouted at her, "Lame Mitza, lame Mitza!" She knew that all her future now belonged to her Eduard. All her persistence, strength, strong will, and devotion, she dedicated to only one goal: to ease the pain of her son. She had never been attracted to charm of the material world. Only the real values, like love and dedication, made up her life.

If we look closely at Mileva's life, we will see that she simply was giving herself to the others without thinking of it as a sacrifice. She followed the bravery of her ancestors from Šajkaš, thus confirming that it was her destiny to give herself to the others. She respected the past and never talked about it; she never complained about Albert, accepting her bitter fate.

Her heart retained undying values of love. That purest feeling of the soul she dedicated to a new goal: recuperation of her son. It was her most honorable decision.

It is said that one has various opportunities to develop his personality. He is sometimes allowed to choose. Long ago, in Titel, Mileva had chosen the path of science and love. Now, she knew that there was nothing more honourable than the love for children. That was the reason why she was going to hospital, day-in-day-out, for years, and took care of the sick, devoting herself entirely to her sick son Tete.

She wondered, from time to time, "Is not that the ultimate reason why I had been made in this profane world?" Albert had let her take care of the boys long ago. Tete spent a great amount of time in hospital, where some rules had to be obeyed, and there, in solitude, he started to hate his father, who let him down and did nothing to take him out of there. Albert Einstein simply did not care about him. In 1930, Eduard wrote a long letter to his father, a letter full of bitterness and desire for revenge. He blamed his father for his split personality, of which he was rarely aware. Rancor was intermingled with love in the soul of the young man. The love was profound and ill fated, and the rancor reached its climax.

Albert used to say that that schizophrenic streak and other troubles had come from Mileva's family, forgetting that her family had been exposed to devastation and many other troubles during the First World War. Albert Einstein had not come to visit his sick son and ex-wife for years.

The last time Albert Einstein visited his ex-wife was in 1933 in Zurich. She saw him coming silently across the yard. She wanted to go out and meet him, but she was not stable on her legs, so she paused in from of the house, measuring the length of the path her beloved being, whom she had not seen for years, was about to traverse. While she was waiting, she tried to think of something good and to collect herself a bit, but then she realized that her happy moments of mutual work and love with Albert Einstein had gone forever to faraway, unknown worlds. She understood now that her heart had forgotten those great endeavors and great sacrifices and remembered only the love for Albert. She knew that it was the proof of her existence. Only the silent, hidden glint of happy tears could be seen in her eyes. Faint, almost invisible rays lit up Einstein's happy face. He was approaching hastily, and it seemed that he was very eager to meet her. There was a strange look in his eyes, asking forgiveness.

Mileva spoke first. "Welcome. How did you travel?"

Albert answered shortly, "Well. How are you?"

It seemed as if he was at a loss for a moment. Sun was spilling its dazzling light, and Albert was seemingly disturbed by it, starting to blink and shade his face with his hand from so much light. Mileva noticed his embarrassment, so she invited him in the house.

They sat in silence for a long time. These two people knew each other very well. They were able to communicate with a strange language even when they were silent.

After a long silence, Albert started to inquire about the sick boy, Tete. He comforted Mileva, promising to help her as much as he could. He wanted to know how she managed to make ends meet, but she assured him that she was accustomed to live modestly and she did not want to change anything. "I had renounced wealth since we were students and lived poorly but happily." She tried to keep back from Albert all her troubles concerning their sick son. She told him that she had been forced to sell one of the houses she had bought from the Nobel Prize money in order to pay the hospital treatment of their son Eduard. The graying and aging woman timidly kept her "sacrifices" secret. Perhaps it was the reason why they had nothing much to say to each other.

Albert did not want to boast about his scientific successes or to speak about the past and their joint research work.

He visited his son in the hospital, and at dusk, he was prepared to leave. He promised Mileva that he would write to her and visit her sometime if his work obligations allowed him.

Mileva sat calmly, hands in her lap. He inadvertently looked at those hands that had written to him all those calculations; he remembered 'cakes sweet as kisses' that they had made for him and how quickly they had tickled the ivories...*Now, it is only a memory,* thought the old man, with tousled hair reaching his shoulders.

Unexpectedly, he approached Mileva to say goodbye. For a moment, he held her both hands, now clenched into fists. He stepped away a bit, as if he wanted to see her better. Then, he gave her a long look full of tenderness. In the corners of his eyes, there were hidden secret tears. "You will stay my faithful wife forever."

Their meeting was quite friendly. Albert disappeared from Mileva's life forever. All the glory, politics, money, and success went away with him. She gave away all to him.

In Berlin, Albert's life became as bitter as Mileva's life had been many years ago. He was expelled from Germany; the fascists took away all his property, robbed his houses, and everything was falling apart. The time came for him to look for an adopted country.

The night when Albert left, Mileva could not sleep for long. With her dark eyes wide opened, she silently gazed at starry sky, and for a moment, she noticed a falling star. Suppressed memories of the past came back to the old woman's mind, and those pictures of the past were dying out with the falling star, quickly and with no return. She left behind all her secrets. Just for a moment, she thought that Albert had been prepared to ask her for those original writings that she had burnt many years ago. She noticed that it was painful for him to utter the question. Thinking of it, she smiled spitefully and, maybe for the first time in her life, she was satisfied that she had destroyed those letters. Albert Einstein's words arose in her mind: "When I am not with you, I think of you with such tenderness that you can hardly imagine."

Now, when she looked back, after so many years, Mileva could not discern what Albert had really wanted to express with these words—sincere love and devotion or superficiality—but it did not matter for her anymore. She remained lonely, staring at the sky and awaiting the days to come.

Years passed. There was no place for illusions in her soul any longer. She knew what kind of future was destined for her. She looked benevolently at success, statements, and newspaper articles about her Einstein. From time to time, a letter from him would arrive. She always spoke nicely of him, admiring his strength and capability to overcome all the troubles of this world, even the concern about his sick son. He managed to suppress all that and continue to live joyfully and merrily, enjoying all the comforts of life.

Albert Einstein did not get along very well with her elder son, reproaching him that he was under great influence of his wife. According to Einstein's opinion, in marriage one should never say, "My wife and I decided..." He was teaching his son that it was correct to say, "I decided."

The elder son, Hans Albert, was a professor of Hydraulic Engineering at the University of California at Berkeley. He was alienated from his father forever because of the bad relationship between his parents. Einstein explained it by Mileva's big and selfish influence on their son. When, in 1927, Hans Albert married "pure" Frieda, all connections between father and son were broken forever.

When on December 3 (December 20) in 1936, Elsa died, Albert felt quite well, in his usual way, like a "bear in his cave." He did not really sympathize with Mileva or his son. He compared Mileva with the evil sorceress Meden, who was said to have killed her husband and sons (since the fifth century, this sorceress Meden has been regarded as evil and malicious).

Mileva's family from Novi Sad was completely ruined. She did not hear from her brother in Russia at all; he was most probably dead. Her mother and father were dead. Zorka lived alone with fifty-five cats; she was mostly occupied with gardening, enjoying in plants and animals, even talking to them. It was a strange environment and a strange way of living. This girl, once very beautiful, survived all the terror of the First World War. She had seen disfigured faces, legs and arms pulled out, and she bore in her soul all the horror of the war. In her solitude, she found the dark chasm of life. She died in 1938.

That same year, Mileva visited Novi Sad, Kać, and Titel for the last time in her life.

In Novi Sad, she had her godparents, the Gajin family, with whom she was very close. Her father, Miloš, died in February 1922, and her mother, Marija, died in 1935.

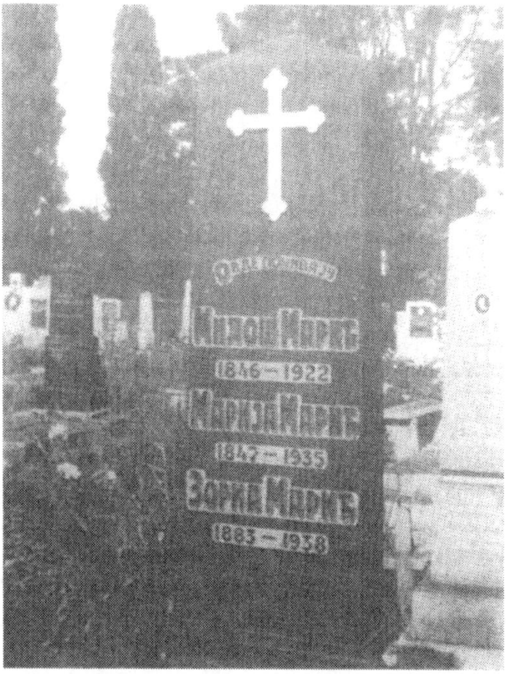

Picture 16: Gravestone of Miloš, Marija, and Zorka Marić

Her brother never called her from Russia. The only thing she heard was that he worked as a professor at a medical faculty. Today, she did not know if he was dead or alive.

The once rather rich estate of the Marić family now was desolate. It was a burnt-out ruin of past times.

The old world of happiness was now unreachable for Mileva. On that day in September, she wanted to be one step closer to those merry past times, but strange, cold dampness crept deep under her skin. She started to shiver, and it prevented her from seeking the lost happiness. When she came to the banks of the Danube with her godmother, she pointed very proudly at the gorgeous bridge that her Hans Albert had made. At least, Mileva thought so, hoping that the name of her son would live forever, connected with the bridge in her beloved homeland. Her eyes were shining then with a strange gleam youth, and she heard for a moment some forgotten sounds, voices, and footsteps. It seemed to her that she heard her dignified father coming, derby hat on his head, gilded stick in his hand, clad in an elegant suit, and she heard his crystal-clear words, saying, "Miloš Marić, retired officer of the royal administration." Father's words were echoing within her soul and mingling with the gentle whispering of her good mother, Marija: "My dear Mitza, my dear child." All that merged into the long-gone past, where she heard the piercing cry of her sick Lieserl. Happiness and sorrow overwhelmed her at the same time; her eyes, hazed with tears, stared for hours at the horizon of Vojvodina.

Mileva tried to revise her life. She could not help but ask who was responsible for the scattered stars fallen from heaven. *They are the only proof that I lived a life,* Mileva thought, catching a petrified tear. She heard her soul weeping for the last time and saying goodbye to the graves of her father, mother, sister, and her dear daughter, Lieserl. Death was now splitting and governing her past life. Sorrow overwhelmed her heart. Silence was all around, and from the closed eyes of Mileva Einstein, tears were running and running. For a long time, she whispered a prayer her grandmother had taught her there, in Titel, where her roots were.

A sparkling light beam appeared from somewhere, woke her up from her painful, dark dreams, and led her to the banks of the Tisa River, where she used to watch boats and to make her sketches and drawings.

She realized then that the river and the play of light were her mental images, her sanctuary, and the symbols of her greatness. That was worth living for. Now, the Tisa River was pompous, vested in golden shirts of fall that reflected in the bluish, glassy water. Light quivered on the yellow leaves in the wind, and everything looked magnificent, unreal. Mileva asked herself if it was the same river where she had daydreamed a long time ago, or if everything had already run out and changed, both people and the river banks…

Just for a moment, it seemed to her that she was a child again and that not all those wrong deeds existed.

With pure soul providence, she remembered her faraway childish dreams about legendary soldiers and leaders: Alexander the Great, Diocletian, Caesar, and others. She knew now that her dream was over.

She left the Tisa riverbanks never to return, though she never lost touch with her homeland. When Yugoslav-Swiss society was established, Mileva became its ardent member.

She never forgot her motherland, those beautiful folk songs she had learnt from her father, all those stories and legends she had heard about the hill Kalvaria in Titel, about Christians arm unbelievers.

Her life was in Zurich now, where her ill son was waiting for her to sacrifice for him. It was her most honorable decision. She thought she could change the destiny of her son, forgetting an old proverb, often seen in the symbols of Renaissance art, saying that destiny is wind blowing in the sails of a boat, while man navigates the direction according to the situation.

During these lonely years, Mileva did not look back. She rarely let herself remember any tiny details connected with her everlasting love. She would sometimes open the big orange box, full of documents and letters, before the day when she gave it all to the fire. Now, there was a small pile of letters, saved by chance, as reminders of the big, fruitful love and past bliss.

When she touched them, memories ran through her mind, and she started to dream about past times, but only for a moment she indulged herself; she actually did not want to be back on the forbidden road.

She took a deep breath and bowed her head in great pain. She began to fade and to deteriorate slowly; it was the last act of her life's play. On the scene of life, she held in her hand the flower of love, whose petals were falling with no movement.

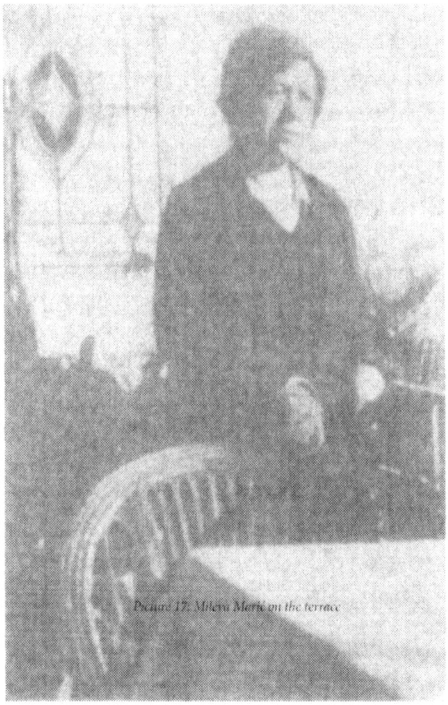

Picture 17: Mileva Marić on the terrace

She leaned her shoulders. Her eyes were wandering somewhere far away, looking for a red fallen petal, taken by the wind into endlessness. She shivered lightly as a spring aspen, and warm tears appeared in the corners of her eyes. She took the old, yellow letter that she had received from her beloved Albert a few years ago, and she read his last sentence numerous times. She found in it the key for her whole life. Albert wrote, "You will see that I will always be faithful to you - in my own way." Mileva understood the gifts of liberated love. Then, she looked back at the past only for a moment and those past days revived. She remembered how the two of them were on the edge of cosmic reunion of destinies, and what he, her great genius, her beloved Albert, had said, holding tightly her hands: "We will be forever united by the same thoughts and the strange, secret love that nobody can take away from us." *Did you remember? You had told me that, a long time ago, many years ago. You had left for good, but I loved you from a distance. Rare were those moments in my life of an old woman when you came to my mind, but only for a moment.*

With her withered, old-woman hands, she caressed the letter tenderly. She did not resist anymore. She knew now that his love and caresses were designed for another woman. It did not bother her; on the contrary, she realized that these remainders of suppressed tenderness could not exist if they were not limited by space and time. She was now enchanted by amorous memories; pale light was covering her face withered with years. Nevertheless, she could not escape from her love for Albert.

That evening, she sat on the terrace until late at night and stared into emptiness. She seemed to follow a thought of hers, though she hid from the world for a long time.

She felt as if she regained her strength and almost forgot that she was old and sick and that, even tomorrow, when the dusk sneaked in quietly, the death would come. The light of her life went out completely. Silence was all around. On the dark sky, the new stars began to live. They were her grandchildren, children of her son Hans Albert: his son Bernhard Caesar and his daughter Evelyn. With hazed eyes, she tried to see the whole space, and saw nothing but the path with no return. She looked back and saw the traces in the past, in everlasting space, hardly visible traces of her soul. For who knows how many times Mileva tried to understand them, yet she tried once more.

In the days to come, she lost her faith and sensed her end would come soon. Solemnly and silently she approached the big, polished mirror of her grandmother, which she had brought from Titel a long time ago. She felt the tarnished wooden frame with a painful hand and sensed the tenderness of some strange, late quivering of lost youth. For a moment, her thoughts were in those long-gone times and she saw in her tearful eyes the images of her mother, father, her sister Zorka, her beloved brother, and her birthplace. She saw all that in the steamy mirror, in lines of her face; she recognized her little dead Lieserl, Hans Albert, and her sick son Eduard. All of a sudden, it was all covered with the ghosts of the past, and they did not let her make out her beloved Albert through the dark. Just for a second, his face flashed in the mirror and then disappeared somewhere, far, far away. It all confused her and she grabbed frame of the mirror so intensively that it broke into thousand pieces. It was the last vigor of Mileva Marić.

Her ancient wisdom, the wisdom that had created the relativity theory, now was influenced by other vibrations; it was concentrated on taking care of the sick son, who spent longer and longer time in the hospital, indulged in fat and laziness.

It appeared that everything was predestined in Mileva's life: misfortune, loneliness, and constant sorrow. With superhuman efforts, being herself ill, she visited her son in the hospital every day. She could hardly walk, so she had to lean on houses, trees, and fences; she would stop to rest a bit and she cried, and when she collected some strength she moved on to her destination, which was always the hospital and her son, whom only she took care of. Albert quit doing it long time ago. He did not feel any need to be in touch with his sons. It seemed that he chose some other destination, where he had everything he needed and wanted. Did he betray his family, Mileva and the sons, or did he only realize the difficult situation of a tragic destiny and simply forgot everything, raised himself above all that, using an ancient formula of successful, healthy living, which said, "Only present moment is what really exists…time and space are only dreams"?

The success was the only thing important for him, the power of creation that Mileva possessed that made paths where they did not exist. He forgot everything else.

Albert Einstein was a rich, famous, successful scientist, well known all over the world, with power to control his own life as well as the lives of others.

Mileva was poor, ill, and forgotten, burdened with constant troubles. One day, when she was going to visit her son, she fell and broke her leg. Some people found her lying unconscious on the pavement and took her to the nearest hospital.

Misfortunes never come singly. Mileva could not see the end of her troubles. She sold the house for Tete's treatment, but with lifelong tenant right. However, she was cheated and expelled, so she had to find an urgent accommodation. She did not worry for herself anymore. She knew that the end was near.

She worried about Tete. His father and brother were far away in the States. Who would take care of him when she was gone? On June 4, 1947, Mileva survived a few strokes. The disease progressed. She could not give away her goodness to anybody anymore. Her mercy deceased. Now she cried warm tears of love, which was completely new for her. Fear and sorrow disappeared forever, and she felt profound happiness.

The vision of spiritual gentleness hovered over the poplars, touching whitish, downy clouds and spreading all over the sky above Zurich. Mileva started to shiver, and the paleness of her face turned into grayish, ashy color. Suddenly, her face became enlightened as of a saint. Now she realized that the time came for her to go on that unconditional journey, to leave her physical body and to forget this place, science, sorrow, dreams, and everything in connection with that. She understood that in the sunset of her life there was no place for deceptive dancers, actors, ghosts that used to warn her of fear, sorrow, love, and hope….Only the moments of this worldly life remained, but they were in the shade of the strong stroke (her left side was paralyzed). Her son Tete was beside her. Those days, he was stable, as if God wanted to soothe Mileva. She consoled herself with the words, "Look, my Tete is fine now." Nevertheless, his bodyguard was watching him from a distance all the time. In her hospital bed, Mileva got a new task that demanded of her to reject this worldly life and to dive into the depth of her divine being, which gave her the opportunity to achieve the perfect calmness before she was gone into whiteness of divine power.

The winding road of the soul was now far behind her. She forgot everything that had appeared before her earlier—her life, experience, wisdom, and sorrow; she knew that she was about to leave this world and that her soul would not turn back anymore. She would bring with her only one thing that filled every corner of her heart, and that was eternal, endless love.

She lay in her hospital bed quietly and motionlessly, perfectly calm and happy. She would open her dark eyes just for a while, and they cast a silent, dim light on her withered face on which one could read the new path of divine truth. However, it was only a part of a symbolic dream, where Mileva whispered noiselessly, “I am so happy today.”

Several minutes after that, sounds of stirring and loud tranquility came from the bed where Mileva was lying, followed by a discontinuous sentence. “Albert, you are my only love. Tell our sons that I love them with the greatest love of another.”

Eduard held his mother’s hand and looked at her with curiosity and fear, not understanding her farewell words. He was silent!

Mileva’s soul slowly merged with a small circle of whitish light of some other reality. When it looked like she was dead, she opened her eyes again, smiling gently and, almost happily, said, “This is the climax of my dream, I am dying…I love you, my son. May God protect you.”

In dead silence that filled the hospital, Mileva’s soul set off for the heavens full of light, for the world not seen by human eyes. It was the sign that she was not among the living anymore and that her mission of scientist, wife, and mother who loved with pure love was complete. She disappeared inaudibly, as a breath.

It was August 4, 1948. Mileva Einstein left this world.

The journey of her soul was over. It travelled from the lower to the higher forms of a perfect being that entered the eternal soul of the divine world. That night, the sky was covered with stars. Far away in the sky, one star had different colour, the colour of celestial beauty. It cast on the Earth some mysterious rays of light that passed the farewell message full of love to nobody else but her beloved Albert.

In one of those days, from the empty space of the Universe, a thought stirred and turned into Albert Einstein’s words: “The value of a man resides…at the first place in how much he gives his thoughts, feelings, and deeds to the benefit of the others. Only a life lived for others is a life worth while.”

Only for a moment, there was a luminous light in Albert’s heart, which smoldered and, soon, turned the past into smoky sooth and emptiness. Mileva Einstein did not exist any longer. All that energy thoughts, scientific achievements remained in the eternal world, and her physical body was modestly buried in Zurich’s cemetery. Many secrets left this world with her. The property that remained after her was rather poor. Ironically but with relief (because the original manuscript of the Relativity Theory was not found), Albert commented on a small sum of money that Mileva had managed to save: “It is a funny thing in all that tragedy: Mileva behaved as a typical Serbian, farmer’s daughter….”

Albert Einstein felt the need to be alone. "Glass wall between an individual and the others," he had written long ago, in 1922, in his diary. He had long ago built the thick wall around himself, and he was safe there in his solitude.

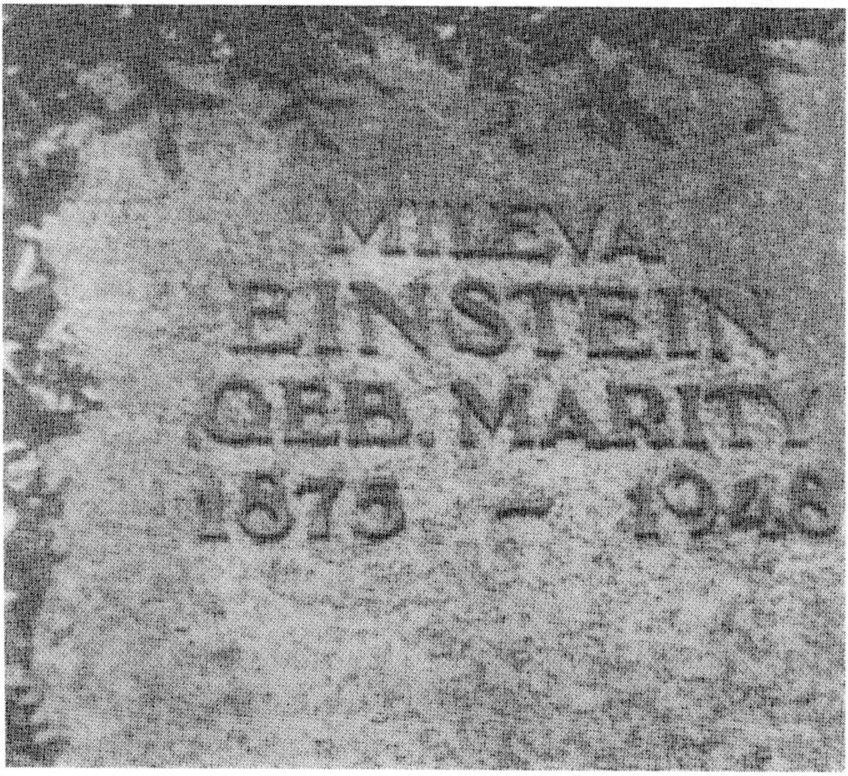

Picture 18: The tombstone of Mileva Marić

Those days in warm August 1948, when Mileva died after a long illness, he felt with his entire being the silence and the endless peace he yearned for all his life.

He was not disturbed by anybody's voice anymore.

All of a sudden, a calm and sticky August day turned into a rainy, gray, and gloomy infinity. Albert Einstein listened to the raindrops bluntly hitting the pavement. The sound of rain was like a blurred memory coming from afar, slowly and painfully. Mileva took the secret of the original manuscripts to the grave with her (all written documents from that period disappeared; *The New York Times* wrote about it on February 15, 1944). "She took away her great love for me," Einstein contemplated.

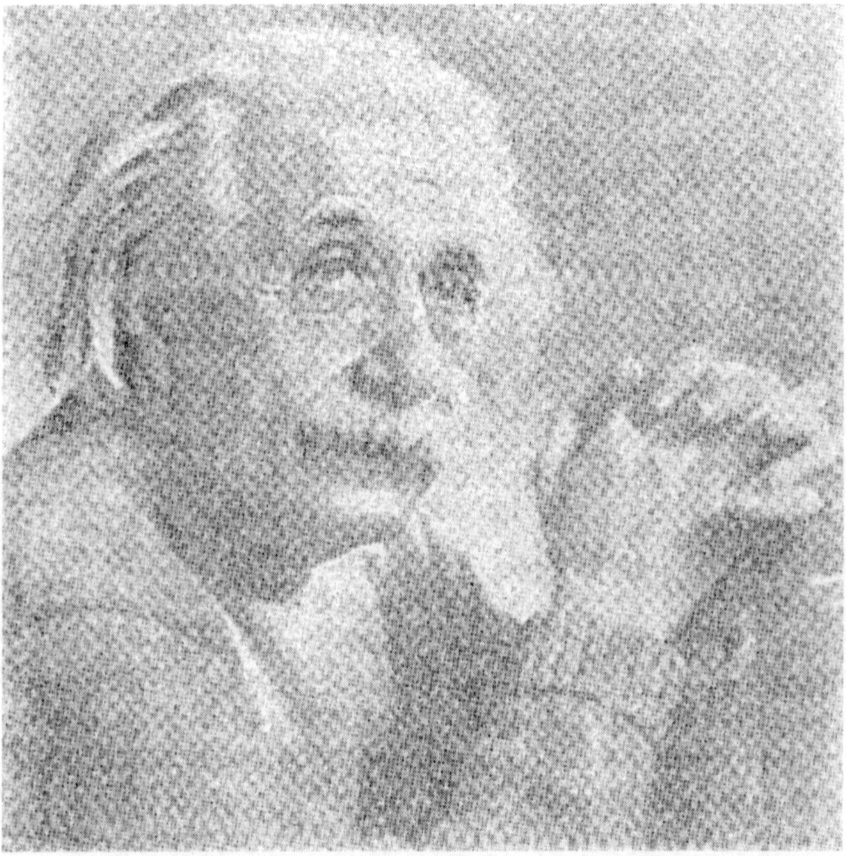

Picture 19: Albert Einstein at Princeton, 1948

He realized at once that the root that fed his entire being was cut off. He did not remember "his ex" anymore. Only present time existed and a curious, vague, almost magical feeling that we sometimes entered the worlds we never imagined we could. Is there a life that begins and ends without tears? *Can a live coal become a flame? Can we live with no shame for tomorrow? It might have turned out differently, but it did not,* Albert Einstein was thinking.

Nothing could be changed anymore. There only remains a question to which we all have to find the answer: why we are here. Mileva was able to find the secret traces of her soul. She knew how to fill every part of her being with unselfish love for her husband and sons, sacrificing everything just for one name: Einstein.

Anyway, that is the way life goes. We do something not knowing the real reason for it. Albert sat alone on a warm August day. He turned his head towards the sun, slicking back his tousled gray hair. His stature appeared as of a child. He smiled, feeling how a part of himself was pulled out from him heading towards blue skies to be merged with Mileva Marić-Einstein into a harmonious, cosmic unity.

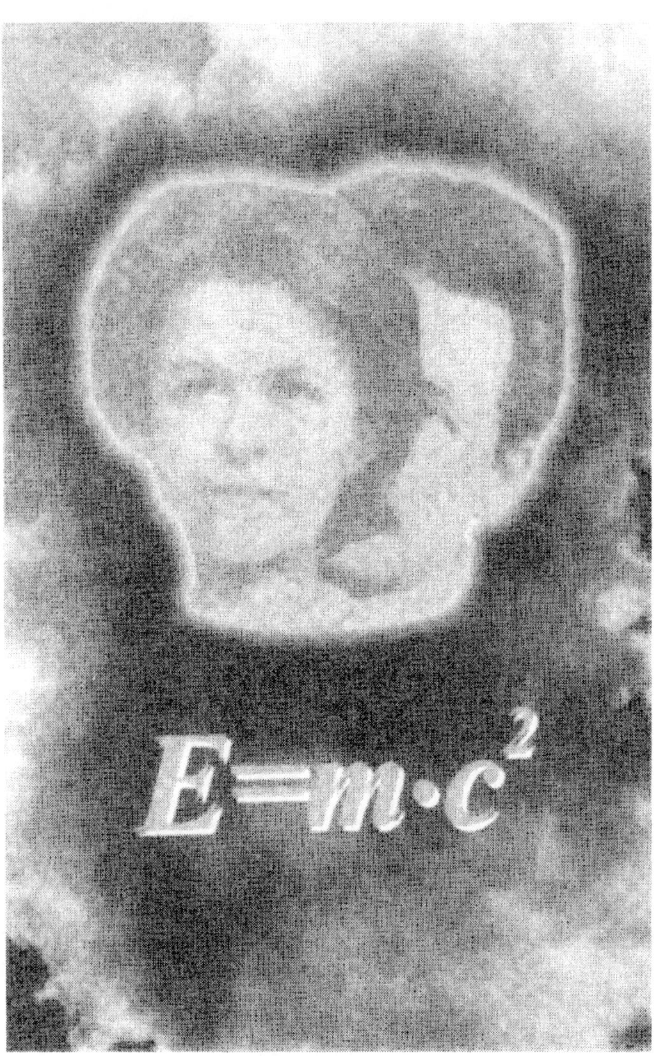

$E=m{\cdot}c^2$

Second coming of Mileva Marić-Einstein

I got up early this morning to watch the sunrise over the bare banks of the Tisa River.

It was the end of May 2002.

I was sitting impressed and enchanted with small particles of flickering light mixed with the whitish cloud heading towards the new embrace of the sky. In that morning magic, I listened to my heart awaiting the heralds of past times.

Suddenly, my eyes stopped on the winding road. It seemed to me that someone was coming, but there was no motion; not even a shadow moved. Purple shadows merged with the gray, dusty road in the weak, dim light, slumbering motionlessly in the morning not yet awoken.

I rubbed my eyes to see better the rising of the sun. Gee, look at this! Out of that shining beauty a creature appeared in the horizon. I almost could not believe my eyes when I saw an old woman limping and approaching me slowly.

She looked absolutely sure about where the road was leading. She knew that she was back in Titel, she knew that she was back in her homeland. Watching the thin line of the horizon, she followed the traces of the past. There were no obstacles ahead of her any longer; there was no celestial punishment of the soul. Her steps followed one another entangled in the first sunbeams.

For a moment, I was not quite sure if Mileva was still walking or she stopped. I was not sure if it was dream or reality. Wind brought to me the words of Mileva Marić Einstein: "The story about a woman started long ago. Nobody can remember when her 'fall' occurred. Now, it is all cured and long forgotten past for me. There is a spark of spiritual history inside my soul. The world will see it in the eyes of my granddaughter Mila, who is the light-bearer of shining beauty, incarnation, and symbol of the things I started long ago in my amorous imagination. Let her receive the message—may her heart live in the rhythm of scientific eternity that merged into endless love, into one unity, into the heart of the world."

After she pronounced these words, Mileva disappeared in the haze as if she had not been there anyway. There was nobody at the triangular crossroad. Golden rays of the morning sun colored the sky like the peacock's tail. I reached for the magic, as if I wanted to grab something above my head, but then I pulled my hands back. Three big white storks crossed my path and disappeared in pale white reeds. They made me feel the waken morning to the full; there were plenty of blossoming water lilies, colorful herbs, and weeping willows packed with green, yellow, and other colourful birds that were joyfully flying over from one tree to another. They tried to outshout one another with their song and suddenly flew off in the freedom of the sky.

Everything became silent, as if nature did not want to wake sleepy Eurydice. At that point, I wished in my soul to hear other forgotten voices from the past. I wished to hear Hans Albert or Edward, but they were not among the living anymore (Hans Albert died in 1973 and Eduard in 1965). The words of Hans Albert remained, when he visited Novi Sad in 1971 and wished that one-room Mileva's house on Kisaćka Street became a memorial room of the first woman theoretical physicist in the world.

Today, there was nobody else except me. There remained only the contours of the eternal world full of charm, magic, and my memories. Here, on the riverbanks, everything was perfectly calm; the river lived its mysterious and beautiful life like before. Sunbeams sparkled on the calm, pale green water that smelt of fish and swamp herbs, together with breeze that I felt now and then on my skin I skimmed the shrubbery, swamp reeds, white and red berries, wide, green wheat fields, and young cornfields, and I felt life growing; I felt the pulse of the rich Vojvodina soil throbbing, of the soil that long ago nurtured the heart of Mileva Marić-Einstein, gentle and strong at the same time.

The sun was above the horizon for a long time. I left the riverbanks impressed and intoxicated with the beauty of nature that looked like a magical paradise. I hurried towards Mileva's Titel. On my way, I was singing a song of Vojvodina players on the "tambura"[1] from the banks of the Danube. I was sure Mileva used to like it, too. Today after so many years, I wondered how this first woman theoretical physicist remained strange and unknown for her fellow countrymen.

And there, in America, Ratko Maglić, professor at the University of Colorado, said, "I saw pictures of Mileva Marić-Einstein on the walls in the corridors of physics department of Colorado College in Colorado Springs. Neither I nor the students of the college can forget her penetrating eyes. Everybody knows about her there."

---

1 A kind of stringed instrument used frequently in Vojvodina - translator's note

I felt happy because of Professor Maglić's words. My heart and dreams were long ago filled with Mileva. I stopped in the middle of a wide street in Titel, which swarmed with jubilant people. I persisted in looking for those familiar eyes on a new face, but I strained my eyes and ears in vain. I asked myself, "Where is now that illusive moment when a girl, walking unsteadily held hands of her mother, Marija, and her father, Miloš? Where is now her caressing voice?"

I waited for her to greet me, but in vain. At that moment, I became aware that I was in front of the Ružićs' house, at the very place where the skies had opened above Mileva.

These are different times, I thought.

Everything had gone with the wind. This was now another Titel. Only the big building of the former barracks of the Šajkaš battalion, where Mileva's father had started his service, stood as a reminder of past times and Mileva's childhood.

A mysterious sorrow captured me, and I tried to conceal it from the others. At that moment, I was aware more than ever that life was passing by us fast, like a snatch. I looked for the bust or for the face of Mileva Marić-Einstein, just to be sure that she still existed.

Somebody startled me with his words: "Her time will come soon. She now lives only in the hearts of the pupils. Our school bears her name: Technical School 'Mileva Marić'."

The unfamiliar voice continued. "Her royal highness, Princess Katarina Karadordević, opens her soul of a benefactor and makes our dreams come true. She builds children's home named after Mileva Marić-Einstein."

That unknown voice brought a strange optimism. All around me and inside me, and inside all of us, there was a nostalgic aspiration that united us all.

"Mileva Marić-Einstein returned in the hillock under the poplar; she is back in her homeland."

She returned, not as an ordinary woman, but as a scientist, as a creator of the relativity theory.

There was a rainbow in the sky, which turned into the gorgeous, dignified silhouette of Mileva Marić-Einstein.

A gentle breeze was blowing over the fields of Vojvodina, carrying the following words into vast space of eternal world.

"This is the second coming of Mileva Marić-Einstein."

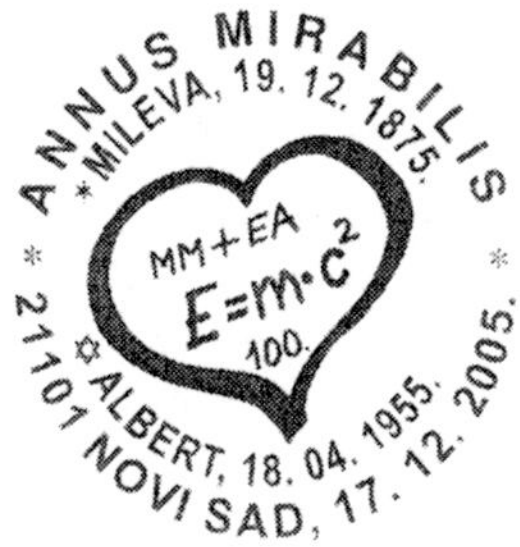

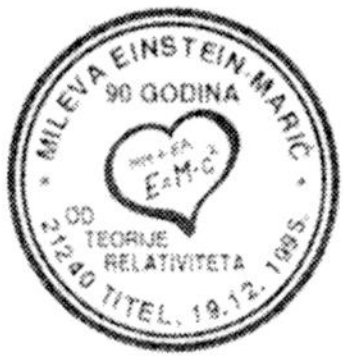

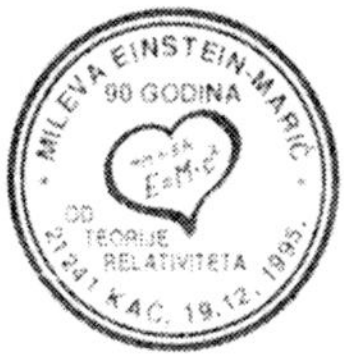

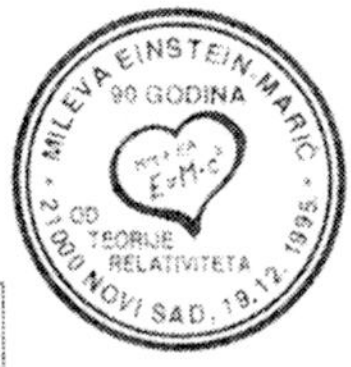

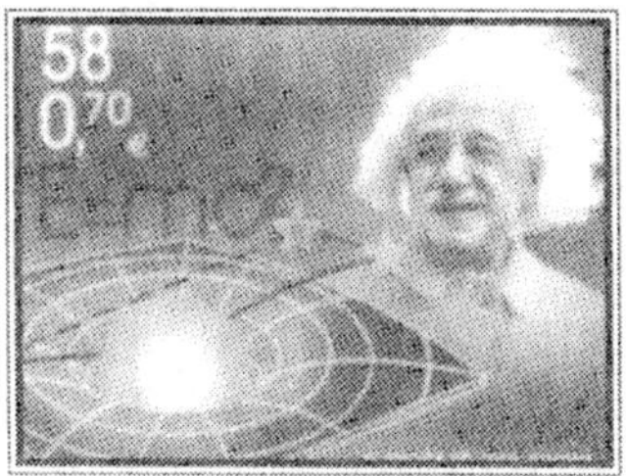

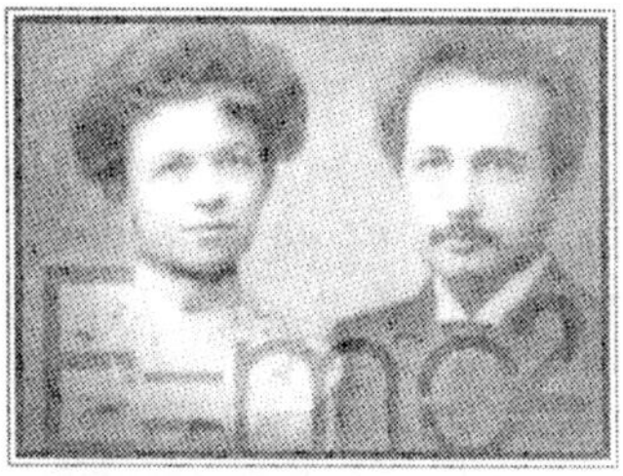

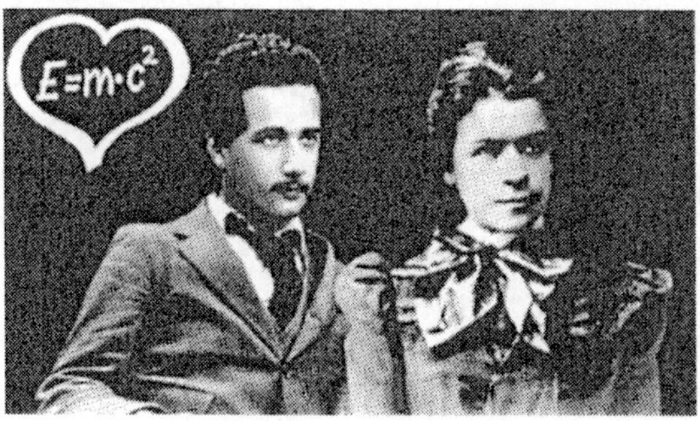

Collect: Dr Aleksandar Mutibarić

The Living Thread

I dreamed of you last night!

There was the thread of name, of feminine fate of birth house, of time-space relative distance and common blood between us. Everything else you bore in a better way and painted in more intensive colors; you heard better, saw clearer, and understood more powerfully—you and your Aunt Milica (your father's sister), my great-grandmother from my mother's side, in some, from this perspective, pre-time that disappears from physical, countable world but never from a mortal's archetypal dreams. I dreamed of you, Mileva, and I know that, in my dream, I asked you some ordinary things—why you gave your sons such high-sounding names for us simple Serbs, Eduard and Albert, instead of naming them simply Milutin and Dragutin. Why did you love another being so much that you withdrew from the pleasant virtual world, from glory and fame, from middle-European dandy-like facade and boredom, although it is possible that God wanted just you as the dancer on this earthly scene? Anyway, it is not important anymore, Mileva; it is I who is tortured with thoughts and impose the question on you. Perhaps you have never heard it. Perhaps you lived a happy, symbiotic life with the man close to your heart and in your big, dark eyes that reflected everything, he was, probably, a bit greater than he really was. It is possible that, writing ciphers or touching the piano keys, you heard a message of the universe that only you could understand and decided to carry it out wisely, silently, patiently, and piously.

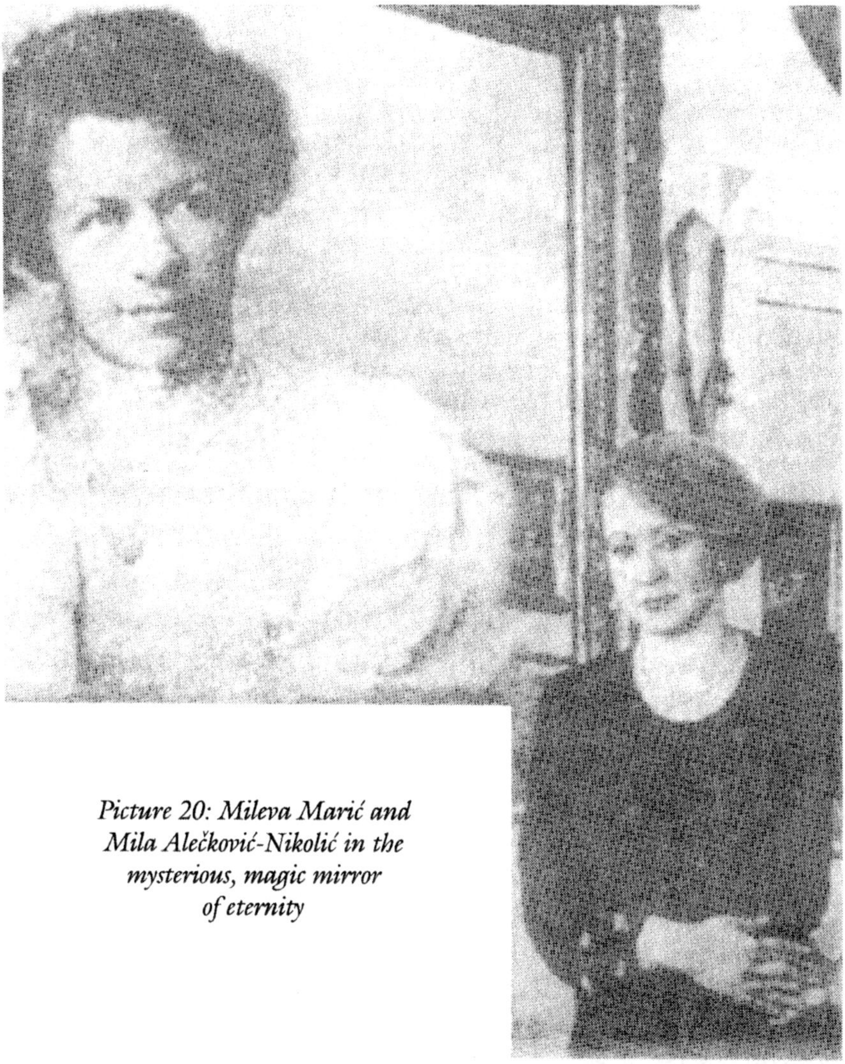

Picture 20: Mileva Marić and Mila Alečković-Nikolić in the mysterious, magic mirror of eternity

The Almighty maybe told you exactly what to do—that you must remain silent and powerful, the bloodstream of another organism and the gray matter of a synapse of another mind, until your own times come. Perhaps you knew all that and you were, anyway, a silent, righteous person walking the Earth, giving meaning to cosmos, loving and giving life to spirit, then to body three bodies.... You stood in my dream so strange, beautiful, and upright, and before you, there were a myriad of transparent, pale faces, but your face was the only visible. Not one of those other faces remained in my memory. I remember only your deep, cloudy eyes and some ancient matriarchal depth and calmness. All the world of acceleration, dynamics, and illusion passed before your pensive eyes, lifted somewhere to the far, galactic ways that only you were capable to understand and from where you observed this short, semi-meaningful life that gains its greatness only when we are not in the same body anymore....Departure from the Serbian, small house in Vojvodina; slim leg of a young woman who walked over the lowland a bit unsteadily; mathematical calculations in an unfamiliar language; unkempt boy in an awkward age whom you adopted as a physical and spiritual mother and his confused thoughts arranged in the order of the special theory; long line of name of wise men who had to persuade a European university of the time that you were a man in woman's body, a kind of genetic error and because of that they should let you, in extremis, to defend what was nastily called "dissertation": three painful childbirths and two unfortunate reincarnations of a genial knot of chromosomes and a psychologically complicated soul; departure of your second self in a distant, different, and new family story; a new feminine breath that was not yours anymore....

Today they say that you that were "the first wife," but you know that you were the first, the last, and the only one....Is it important now, anyway? I saw you in my dream completely absorbed in thoughts and love, but alone; you know that master's calculations must never calculate human soul, and you lived according to that Serbian and Slavic principle.

Do you know, Mileva, that you amaze me, though I have a part of your warm blood, but nothing, actually, of your power? You amaze me and you remain for me the secret that I will solve one day, probably because my dreams are my war allies and because they tell me something I cannot find in any history of relativity.

You are a Serbian woman after all, like Jevrosima, Jefimija, and Milica, and your life can be another "Slovo Ijubve"[2], written in a new, encoded alphabet.

When I was a child, I saw in Novi Sad one of your sons, I am not sure if it was Eduard or Albert, and now I realize that I recognized, in that sad, old face, something unmistakably yours, something that drew back that face from California of Switzerland to the small house in Vojvodina, where he came to do you honor for the last time. He wanted to feel once again the absolute domination of the spirit of a Slavic mother before he disappeared from the physical reality.

I hear again, like in my mosaic dream, the beat of wooden piano keys, which you transform with your long fingers into an omnipotent sound of Jupiter, and I see your awkwardly bound hair, prominent forehead, snub nose, and lowered eyelids.

You told yourself silently, "In this music of my childhood is the calculus I seek. I will finish your equation, Albert, but hear the harmony first and then we will together transform it to a proof. It will last after we leave this world."

---

2 "Slovo Ijubve" – "The Words of Love" - Serbian medieval poem written by Despot Stefan Lazarević (1377–1427), an example of highly cultivated style, inspired and original medieval poetry - translator's note

You closed the piano keyboard, took an invisible object in your hand, and lay down. A crow cawed so loudly that I woke up, startled.

Do not ever leave, Mileva. Stay with us here. Give your name to a street, square, park, to a new little girl, like the one you lost, to another wise and enamored woman, to some new space and time that you, chosen on the reel around the sun, secretly understood before us all.

In the name of mother and daughter and goddess of Holy Spirit, amen.

Love,
Mila[3]

3 Mila Alečković-Nikolić, a psychologist, was a relative to Mileva Marić-Einstein through her mother's (Mira Alečković) mother, Draga.

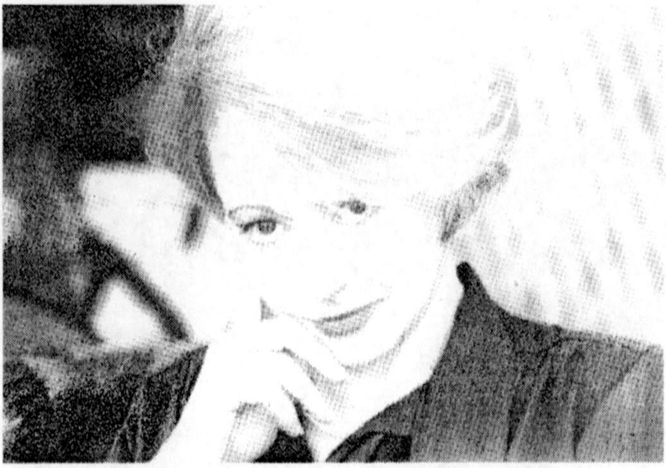

Review

When I saw Svetlana's big, vivid eyes for the first time, at the reunion of Serbian Diaspora, I felt at once that she, in a way, belongs to us, dispersed and reunited Serbs from all over the world, that she can understand us and love us in a special way and that it was not by accident that she came among us and merged with us afterwards.

I did not know then that Svetlana was already leading the correspondence with Mileva Marić, also a providential representative of Serbian Diaspora and Serbian migrations, and that her imaginary conversations with Mileva were considerably in progress, due to the fact that, of course, Mileva "consented" to them. I did not know that Svetlana and Mileva became even closer and that Svetlana was about to say something about it to the world.

Reading this book today, about a woman who found meaning in indifferent calculations and thoughts, I know that this book, after a number of texts and books of the same topic, is written sincerely, without pretentiousness and deeply compassionately.

For Svetlana, Mileva is not a life's "victim," but a strong woman in love.

Svetlana can make difference between a real human weakness and the disguised one that hides great strength and generosity.

Mileva's sacrifice Svetlana sees as a cosmic and bestowed power, and not as hopelessness. She knows that Albert is psychologically weaker and that he, because of his narcissism, cannot see the very essence that his Serbian wife, teacher, mother, and sister will prove. However, Svetlana does not reproach Albert. She says sincerely and simply, "Mileva did not let me."

There lies Mileva's greatest strength that other authors did not observe. As a gift from God, Svetlana gave the right diagnosis at once.

It is possible that all the books written about the silent life of a Serbian woman were written with sincere intentions and with empathy or with admiration and pity at the same time. It seems to me that Svetlana's book is the least programmed and the most authentic in identification with other beings. It was written according to the feelings of a person who was given an "assignment," who heard the call and the order to write.

Only that way one can explain the fact that Svetlana lived again every instant of Mileva's intricate life—from awareness of a lost baby girl, animosity of her mother-in-law, confused family in Vojvodina, a hard night's work over calculations, to awareness of human defeat and absurdity of everything that is not colored with passionate love, the only thing that, in our short life, makes a clear connection between causes and consequences.

Albert's stimulus was ratio, and Mileva's was emotions, as Svetlana shows us. However, Mileva, not Albert, was the one who reached the highest point of rationality.

The author of the book, like all other people who deal with transcendental things, is not lured in the traps of everyday life.

Mileva's life is full of grayness, but there is a palette of colors on some other, higher level, which is so clear to the author. In the evidence of the book, she does not try to "psychoanalyze" everyday life, but she writes fluently, easily, and simply; in the darkness of semiconsciousness and as if through hypnotic pictures, she puts on paper what she dreamed of, what was "shown" to her and what was whispered to her.

In this book, Svetlana told us what we knew and what we did not know about Mileva Marić. However, she told us the very essence, and that is, that you should not write a book about a character you do not love, and if you did not enter fully in his time, his life, his workroom, his notes, and his inner self. Biographies should be written only through identification, and if it lacks, the book should not be written at all.

This is my modest "moral" of a psychologist, made after I read a good book.

The book about Mileva is, as I see it, the work of sincerity, identification, annulment of chronologic distance, and strong spiritual advocacy.

Svetlana Alter tried to be Mileva's second self in some other time, to be her alter ego.

She succeeded because Mileva already agreed to it.

Dr Mila Alečković-Nikolić

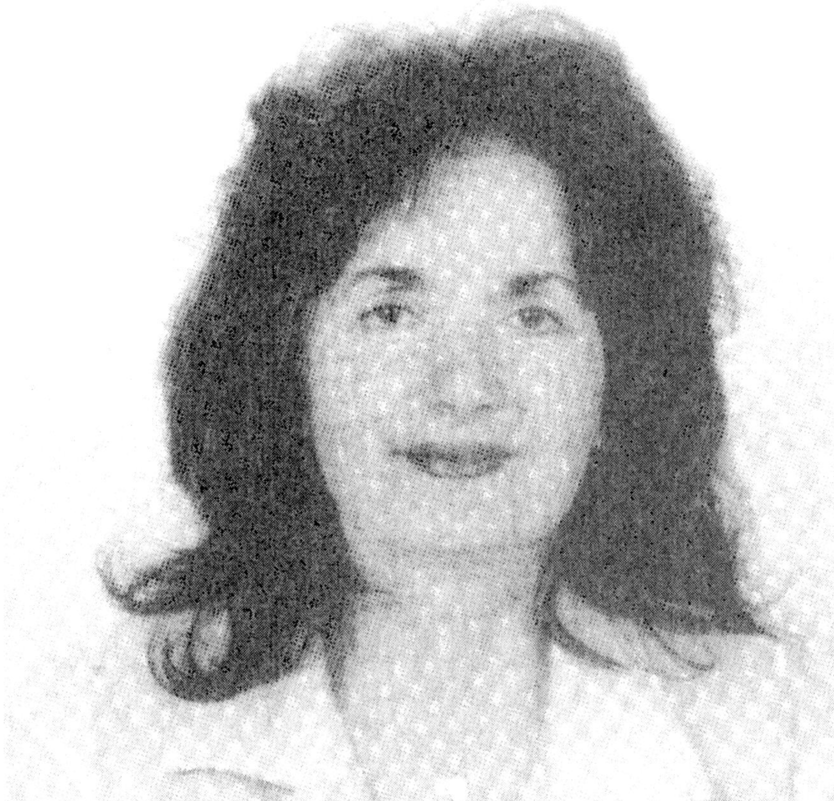

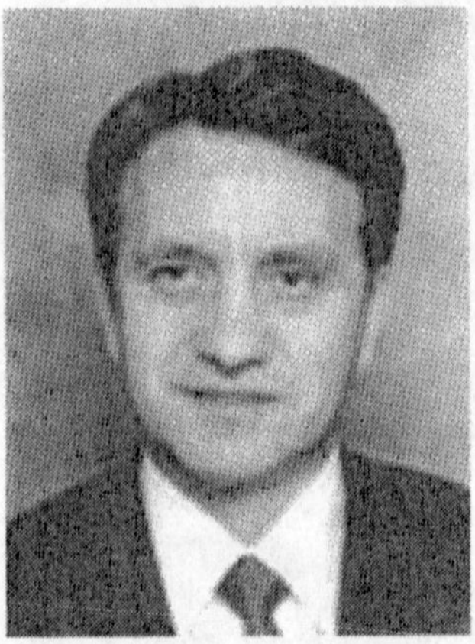

Desko Nikitovic Consul General of Serbia and Montenegro in Chicago

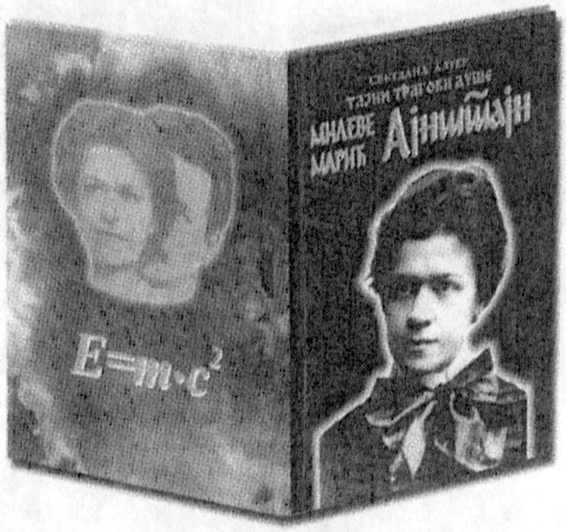

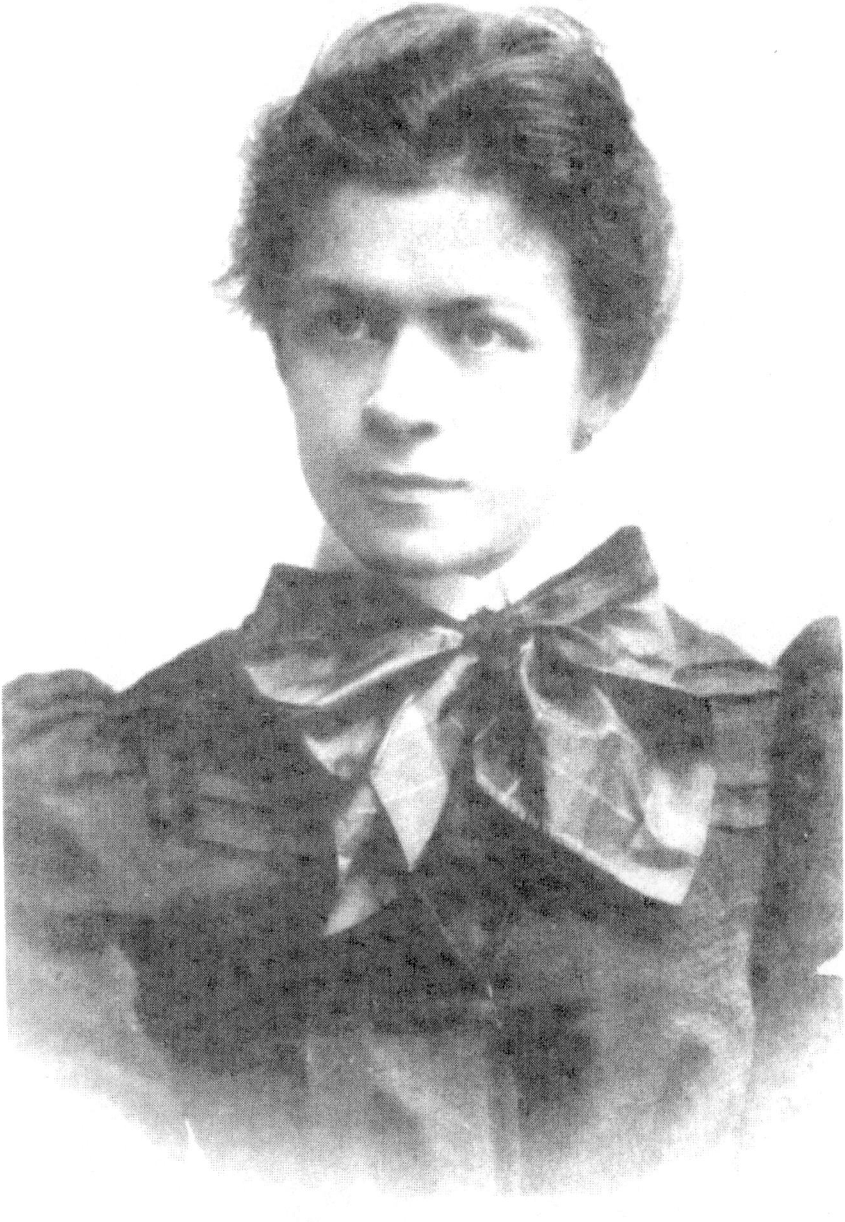

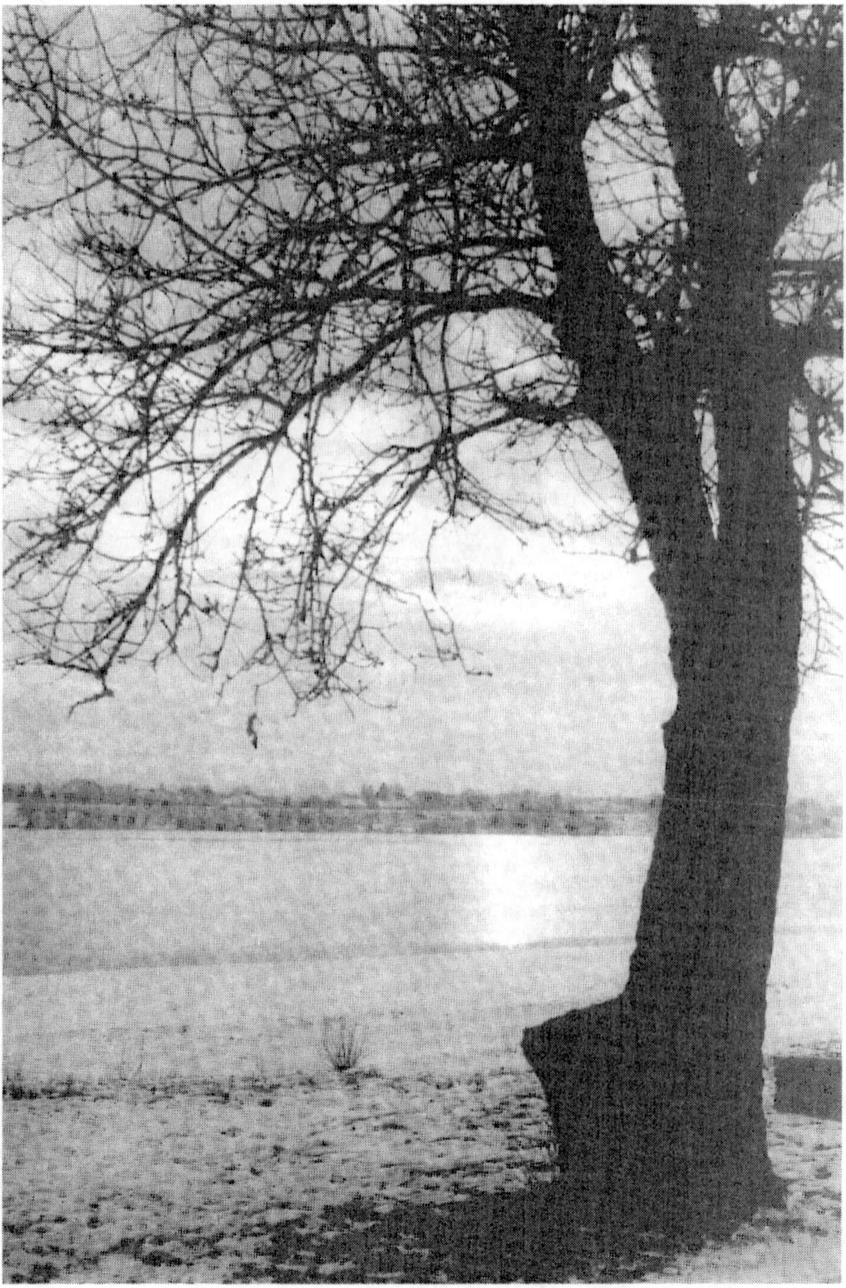

CPSIA information can be obtained at www.ICGtesting.com
Printed in the USA
LVOW07s2018040116

469060LV00025B/1434/P

9 781434 928030